Marcia
118 Falconer St
Fredsburg N.y.

Some trails are happy ones, others are blue. It's the way you ride the trail that counts; here's a happy one for you.

Dale Evans, "Happy Trails"

He was King of the Cowboys. She was Queen of the West. To us, they were just
Mom and Dad and living with them was almost as rowdy as a Saturday matinee . . .

with
Karen Ann Wojahn

Regal Books
A Division of GL Publications
Ventura, California, U.S.A.

All Scripture, unless otherwise noted, is from the Authorized King James Version. Scripture marked *NIV* is from the *Holy Bible, New International Version.* Copyright © 1973, 1978, 1984 International Bible Society. Used by permission of Zondervan Bible Publishers.

Published by Regal Books
A Division of GL Publications
Ventura, California 93006
Printed in U.S.A.

Library of Congress Cataloging in Publication Data.

Rogers, Roy, 1946-
 Growing up with Roy and Dale.

 1. Rogers, Roy, 1912-   . 2. Rogers, Dale Evans. 3. Rogers, Roy, 1946-
 . 4. Christian biography—United States. I. Wojahn, Karen Ann. II. Title.
BR1725.R63R64   1986   791.43'028'0922 [B]   86-6524
ISBN 0-8307-1158-9

1 2 3 4 5 6 7 8 9 / 90 89 88 87 86

To the loving memory
of Robin, Sandy, and Debbie,
who taught me compassion;
To Tom, Cheryl, Linda, Marion and Dodie,
who rounded out my life;
To Mom and Dad
who taught me to know and love God,
showed me right from wrong,
and encouraged me to be myself.

Acknowledgments

To Karen Ann Wojahn, my alter ego, for being so much like me that it's scary. Thank you for getting out of me things only an alter ego can and for being an intelligent and loving person with the insight to see the other side of what I was saying.

Also, to Karen's sister, Susan Dix Hodge, who spent hours and hours at a word processor transcribing the many hours of taped interviews into some sort of sense.

And to my storage barrel, for supplying me with the countless photos of my past that helped me stir up so many memories.

And finally to my wife, Linda, and my children Shawna, Kelly and Dustin, for giving me up for many hours while this story of my life unfolded.

And to my Lord and Saviour, for giving my life some sort of direction and purpose.

Dad and I (age two) on location of the Roy Rogers and Dale Evans Show.

Preface

It was an exciting time to grow up. World War II was finally over, the taste of victory fresh. Right had been vindicated, wrong had been routed, and America lived in an age of hero worship. The villain always failed, and the hero—on the side of law and order, of righteousness and integrity—always triumphed in the end.

It was the Hollywood heyday of Clark Gable, Gary Cooper and Cary Grant, and though they were the ones who dominated the marquee and carried away the Oscars, the Saturday afternoon matinee usually featured the shoot-em-up, ride-em-out, rough-and-tumble Western. The stuff of such dreams made Gene Autry, Hop-A-Long Cassidy and Roy Rogers the idolized, romanticized and fantasized heroes of America's theater-going children.

When television invaded the American home, these cowboys became the friends of every boy and girl in the nation, and for 10 consecutive years, my dad was named Cowboy of the Year. By the mid-fifties, Roy Rogers, the "King of the Cowboys" and Dale Evans, the "Queen of the West" were among the most beloved of all children's entertainers, playing to standing-room-only-crowds wherever they made personal appearances.

After more than half a century in show business—and nearly three decades since their television program went off the air—my parents continue to be recognized, honored, and loved wherever they go, and they continue to receive fan mail week after week.

So familiar is my dad's voice that people come out of shops along city streets to greet him. They approach him in restaurants and department stores, and they run up to him when they chance to meet him at the Roy Rogers and Dale Evans Museum in Victorville, California.

One afternoon Dad was walking with some friends through the display area of the museum and a tourist spotted him. "Roy Rogers!" he shouted. Before Dad knew what was happening, the six-foot-plus mountain of a man had lifted him off the ground and twirled him around!

Suddenly realizing what he had done, the man stopped, put my dad down, and blushed. "I'm so sorry, Roy," he stammered. "I was so glad to see you in person after all these years, for a minute there, I forgot I wasn't a kid anymore."

My folks always seem to bring out the hidden children in people. Mom continues to travel all over the country in response to hundreds of requests annually for her to speak. People light up like candles when they see her. She's everybody's sister, everybody's mom. In a sense, that's because if she's anything, she's a mother. She marks time by what happens to her children and grandchildren.

Wherever I go people ask me what it was like, growing

up the way I did. What does it mean to be Roy Rogers, Jr.? It's a question I've mulled over for more than 30 years, and the answer is full of paradoxes.

No matter what their life-styles are, most children think of their lives as "normal" and "ordinary." It's only in retrospect that we begin to see what was unique or special or different about our particular families, how we did things, and how childhood events affect our adulthood. I was certainly no different in that respect.

To me, Dad was just Daddy. He played with us and took us on vacations, and he spanked us when we needed it. He went to work like other dads, but his work was in the field of entertainment. I never thought of my mother as anything but Mom, and although working mothers were unusual in those days, I can't remember thinking of my mom's work as being anything special.

Other people *did* think of my parents as special, though; consequently they thought of me as unusual, too. There is a certain mystique about people in show business, and that mystique raises many questions. Even today, my own three children are often confronted with questions like, "Do you ever get to go over to your grandparents' house?" Of course they do, but people tend to expect us to depart from the ordinary.

Naturally there *are* some differences between how we lived and how others did, but for us, those variations were insignificant. Perhaps because my parents never forgot the poverty of their own backgrounds, they determined to give their children values and standards that would see us through the tough times. Perhaps because our family came from different heritages and varied backgrounds, we could see things from a wider perspective. Perhaps it's because there were so many of us; children can be a great equalizer. Whatever the reasons, we didn't *feel* different.

11

Our family has known terrible grief in the face of unspeakable tragedy, but we have also known what it is to be happy and loved, nurtured and secure. What we thought about the day-to-day events of our lives is probably much the same as what other children thought. Like them, we had television heroes like Superman and the Cisco Kid and the Lone Ranger and Sky King, and we imagined ourselves in wonderful make-believe settings.

We felt lonely and afraid sometimes, like other children, and we looked forward to Christmas and birthdays and vacations from school. When we were happy we laughed, and when we were hurt, we cried. Our feelings were no different from those any other human being would have, and our memories are not unlike those of most people who grew up during the post-war baby boom era.

Yet my parents are ordinary people who have lived extraordinary lives. Because of this, my life, too, has been a blend of the ordinary and the extraordinary. But it isn't just *my* life I want to share with you. It's the life I shared with my eight brothers and sisters, and in a sense, the life I shared with thousands of other children who grew up with Roy Rogers and Dale Evans.

one

Latch-key kids. Hired baby-sitters. Working mothers. Divorce. Remarriage. Stepchildren. Death. Hollywood. Fame.

Any one of these elements can—and often does—provide ample climate for child abuse, juvenile delinquency, rebellion or misery. Any combination of two or more of these factors invites disaster, but when all are present, the total spells doom. By any stretch of the imagination, our family should have been a textbook case of how *not* to succeed with children.

Mom had been divorced before she married Dad, who was a young widower with three small children. Most days, both of them were already on the set before sunup, and it was dark when they returned home at night. Personal appearance tours took them away from home for weeks at a time. The odds were against them. The odds

13

were against us all, against our making it as a family.

I can still feel myself bump-bump-bumping down the stairs of our home in the southern California community of Hollywood Hills. Too little to walk down the stairway, I bumped down on my bottom. Our house had been built by the late Noah Beery, and it sat up on a hill about a mile or so north of Hollywood and Vine. It was a large, rambling Spanish-style house, a nice house, and I liked it there.

Among the things I liked best were the animals. Dad loves animals, too, and we always had lots of them everywhere we lived. When he married Mom, she got more than a husband. It was definitely a "package deal," and the package included three children, 30 hunting dogs, innumerable horses, and more than 200 homing pigeons!

Dad kept the pigeons in a large coop at the end of the carport. When he worked on location, he often took his homing pigeons to the set and released them. One of the hired men clocked them as they came in.

Behind the pigeon coop was a fenced area where Dad and my grampy had built a pond for goldfish. Grampy Slye was only about 5'8" tall, and he looked a lot like Dad—or, to be precise, it was the other way around. My grandmother (we called her Mammy) used to say that when her husband and her son smiled, no one could see their eyes. Because finely chiseled Choctaw features gave both men a permanent squint, they always had the appearance of someone looking into the sun.

Dad's folks had moved out to California from Ohio in the early 1930s, just before Dad decided to try his hand at show business. Grampy always had something to do, like selling eggs or working with chickens or the pigeons. He had a little garden, and he raised grapes.

My grandmother, Mattie Slye, had always had difficulty walking, ever since childhood. After their move to

14

California, Dad took her to some specialists who said she had apparently had polio as a child. When Dad started making money, he was able to buy her a leg brace, which gave her more mobility. Mammy was tiny, barely five feet tall, but she was tough.

She had a doll collection that Dad started for her. He sent dolls from all over the world. Any time we children would get near the dolls, she'd say, "You get near my dolls, child, and I'll snatch you baldheaded!"

She reminded me of a bulldog—you could pet it and like it, but never turn your back on it. I loved her, and I really liked her, but I was a bit afraid of her, too.

Mammy and Grampy were unpretentious people, and even when Dad invited them down to the movie set, they would always say, "No. No, Leonard, we don't want to get in anybody's way." To them, Dad was always Leonard. They never thought of him as Roy Rogers. It wasn't until after he married my natural mother that Dad legally changed his name from Leonard Slye to Roy Rogers.

I don't know very much about my natural mother. Her name was Grace Arlene Wilkins, but Dad always called her Arlene. He met her in 1933 while he was doing a radio show in Roswell, New Mexico. Money was tight during those days of the depression, and for weeks Dad and the other fellows in his group had been hunting rabbits and shooting hawks off of telephone wires in order to eat. There's not much meat on those wild black birds, and Dad still says the gravy was so tough it could bend a fork!

One day the boys were so hungry they didn't think they could make it. Dad told the radio audience that he'd really like a lemon pie, and the next day Arlene appeared at the stage door with two of them. Although Dad was delighted with the pastry, his eyes feasted on the lovely ash blonde who brought them. Tall—about 5'9"—soft-spoken and gentle, this girl captured his heart right away. Even today, he and those who knew her describe my mother as a great lady.

For the next three years they wrote letters back and forth while he and the newly-formed Sons of the Pioneers were on the road. He stopped in Roswell whenever he could. They married in June of 1936—about a year before my dad signed his contract with Republic Pictures and found himself plunged into stardom.

My natural mother could sing and play the piano, but she was never really interested in Hollywood or in the "cowboy" scene. I've only seen one photograph of her in western attire. Although she did go along with Dad on his personal appearances, she really wanted only two things: to make a home for Dad, and to have children.

By 1940, when no babies came, she and Dad began to consider adoption. Dad had always played orphanages and hospitals, and he often told her about the babies he'd seen. One little girl in a Kentucky orphanage had just about broken Dad's heart when he went there for a visit. She had grabbed him and refused to let go, begging him to take her with him. He never forgot that.

During one particular trip back to California, he stopped in Dallas to talk with Bob O'Donald and Bill Underwood, who owned theaters there. In the course of their conversation, Dad mentioned his thoughts about adopting a baby, and one of them said, "You're talking to the right people, Roy. We're on the Board of Directors of Hope Cottage."

Hope Cottage was less than a mile away, and Dad could hardly wait to walk into the nursery. There were 42 babies, but when one little blonde head popped up, Dad melted. It was Cheryl Darlene. When Cheryl was four months old, Dad brought her home.

As happens sometimes, once Cheryl was settled in, my mother became pregnant with Linda Lou, and then, four years later, with me. Although my dad was uneasy about it, the doctor decided my mother should have a Caesarean section, and so I was born on October 28, 1946 at Madison Hospital in Los Angeles. Radio stations and newspapers all over the country announced, "The King of the Cowboys Has a Prince!"

Dad had been on a personal appearance tour in Chicago, and he arrived at the hospital not long after I was born. He wanted to call me Dustin Roy, but he changed his mind. Instead, he named me Roy Rogers, Jr., but he always called me "Dusty." He'd had his own name legally changed in 1945, just a year before I was born, or I'd probably have ended up being named Leonard Slye, Jr.

My mother was recovering nicely from the birth, but in those days the doctors didn't realize how important it is to have the patient up and walking after surgery. Early the following Sunday morning, November 3, a blood clot loosed itself in her blood stream and went to her brain. The hospital called my dad, and he and Grandma Wilkins, her mother, broke all the speed limits to get to the hospital. My mother died just as they arrived. I was only six days old.

Dad was overwhelmed. Long hours of daily work on a picture followed by extensive personal appearance tours made it impossible for him to be both mother and father to three small children. A string of housekeepers and nurses didn't seem like a good answer, either.

Dad's stand-in, Whitey Christiansen, told him that his mother had just lost her husband. She could move in and help with the girls and take care of me. In addition to Mrs. Christiansen, Dad also hired a nurse, Virginia Peck. I bonded to Virginia right away because she was very much a "mommy." During the next nine years, she permanently endeared herself to me.

For two years Dad had been making movies and personal appearances with Dale Evans, and during the 13 months following my mother's death, their professional relationship blossomed into friendship. I suppose nobody was really surprised when the team who had worked together so successfully at the box office decided to commit their lives to each other.

The decision to marry Dad was not an easy one for Dale. She had a 20-year-old son, Tom Fox. Her marriage at the age of 14 to Tom's father ended in divorce, and Dale's mother had assumed much of the responsibility for Tom's upbringing.

Dale felt terribly guilty about Tom, but she knew she couldn't give him the kind of care he needed. In those days the studios did not like their stars to be married or to have children. Dale's background, if publicized, could have hindered her career. For some time, she kept Tom a secret, although she had remarried. By the time she signed her contract with Republic Pictures, the demands of a Hollywood life-style had taken its toll on that marriage, too.

With the failure of her marriages behind her, the likelihood of succeeding in a marriage with three stepchildren seemed impossible. When Dad asked her to marry him, she promised God there would never be a divorce. She could not face the responsibility of putting Cheryl and Linda and me through the trauma of adjusting to yet another stepmother.

Mom always told us her life was a mess until she was 35 years old, when God used my stepbrother Tom to turn her life around. About to be married himself, Tom told her, "Mom, you are bound to fail again and again until you turn your life over to Christ. No marriage can really succeed

Grandpa Slye, a playful Lana and I in front of our Hollywood Hills home.

Mortimer Snerd (Edgar Bergen) delights two small fans: Candice Bergen (center) and me at my second birthday party.

without a personal relationship with Jesus."

The night Mom and Dad were married, she asked God to give her the strength and courage to establish a Christian home for us. "Lord," she said, "I don't want them to go through what Tom went through." Throughout the years she has reminded us again and again that God's grace is what has seen us through. The odds were against us, but God was with us.

Mom and Dad were married on New Year's Eve, 1947. Cheryl was seven, Linda Lou five, and I was 14 months old. Soon afterwards, we moved into the house in the Hollywood Hills. What I remember about those early days comes only in snatches—events that impressed me, perhaps, because they were out-of-the-ordinary and even adventuresome for a toddler.

One of my most vivid memories is of an autumn day when a Western musical group was rehearsing at the house. My sisters were at school that day, and I rode my tricycle on the covered patio just outside the kitchen. It was a warm, balmy day, and the air had a rich, woodsy fragrance. The sky was clear in the morning, but it began to darken, and a reddish glow surrounded us. Suddenly I heard someone shout, "Fire!"

I ran out to the yard. The members of the group were grabbing hoses. A canyon fire had made its way past our property line. It was impossible for the fire trucks to get to the back side of the property, so they came through the electric gates at the front, and up the long driveway to the large parking area that doubled as a tennis court.

While we waited for the fire department, the boys climbed up on the block wall that separated our yard from the underbrush. They were hosing the fire, and I wanted to help. I ran into our little kitchen, grabbed a loaf of bread and tore back out to the yard. I rushed up to where two of the boys were, and I began to throw pieces of bread on the fire. I can see the headline now: *Roy Jr. Invents Toast.* Someone jerked me back, and before long, the fire was out and things were back to normal.

But around the Rogers's house, "normal" was only a brief interlude between calamities. Not long after the fire, a near-tragedy happened to my older sister, Cheryl, who must have been about nine at the time. Mom and Dad were away, and Virginia was taking care of us, as usual.

Our front door was a big, glass-paneled dutch door, and the top half always stuck. One day Cheryl ran down to the gate to get the newspaper, and on the way back up she began to roughhouse with Joaquin, one of our dogs.

Joaquin was a weimaraner—a wonderful large gray sporting dog with short hair, a cropped tail and ears that hung like pendulums. Joaquin was Cheryl's special pal. He listened to all of her sad tales sympathetically, but he also loved to play.

Just as Cheryl ran up to the deck of the porch and put her hand on the glass pane, Joaquin jumped in the middle of her back, pushing her hand right through the door. The shattered glass opened her arm to the bone.

Virginia and Linda and I were in the kitchen when we heard Cheryl's screams. We ran through the double doors to the dining room and rounded the corner to the entryway. Blood spurted everywhere as Cheryl held her arm, screaming. Virginia whipped her apron off and pressed it against the wound.

"You're going to be all right, Honey," she kept telling Cheryl. "Linda Lou, run upstairs and get me a couple of clean towels from the dresser in the bathroom. There, there, Cheryl. Shhh. It's all right."

Virginia wrapped Cheryl's arm in the towels Linda brought her, then set her on the steps while she phoned

21

the doctor. Cheryl was still crying as we all piled into Virginia's car and took Cheryl to the doctor. It took 45 stitches to close the wound, and Cheryl still carries the scar.

By spring Cheryl's accident and the fire were fading memories. I was about three, and the most important thing in my life was playing outside. Easter Sunday was no different, and I didn't even hear Mommy tell me to stay on the patio after she dressed me for Sunday School.

I stood on the patio for a few minutes, looking out into our huge backyard. I wondered if the Easter bunny had put any eggs out near the goldfish pond. I wandered out past the pigeon coop toward the pond, and then I spotted Lana, Joaquin's mate.

"Come on, Lana!" I shouted. I clapped my hands like I'd seen Dad do. "Come on, girl!"

A big gray sporting dog, Lana was an excellent pet, but she was as playful as a puppy that morning. Panting wildly, she tore up to me and sniffed at my face, then nosed me along backwards a few steps until I lost my balance. Before I knew it, Lana was barking at me and I was sitting in the pond.

By that time, Mom and Dad noticed I was missing, and they came running out past the carport and the pigeon coop.

"Dusty!" Mommy screamed. "Oh, Papa, he's in the pond! He'll drown! Get him out!"

As soon as they realized I was all right—just covered with mud and muck—Mommy scolded me.

"Don't go near the pond anymore, Dusty! Look at you! What a mess. Now you'll have to wear your old clothes to Sunday School. You *scared* me!" But Mommy didn't sound scared to me. She sounded *mad*. She rattled off her lecture in rat-a-tat style as she marched me onto the patio and into the little kitchen next to Daddy's study.

22

In the kitchen she peeled off my little Western suit and sopping boots and socks so I wouldn't drip, then dried me off with a kitchen towel. Swooping me up in her arms, she rushed through the double doors to the dining room, rounded the corner to the entryway and tore past the little wet bar to the stairs. My bedroom was at the top of the stairs, and she plopped me on one of the beds in my room.

"Linda! Cheryl!" she called. "Dusty's made a mess of himself again. Are you ready for Sunday School? I'll be just a minute!"

"I can't get my new bonnet tied, Mommy," Linda called. "Cheryl helped me buckle my Sunday School shoes, though."

"Thank you, Cheryl!" Mommy pulled out a fresh set of underwear from the dresser drawer and grabbed my old Sunday clothes from the closet.

"Come on, you little stinker," she said. "This will make you happy—now you get to have your face washed and your hair combed all over again!" She maneuvered me into the bathroom and pulled a wash cloth from the built-in dresser.

By this time I was cold, so I eased over to the wall heater while Mom turned the porcelain spigot on the old-fashioned sink. Tiled halfway up the wall with wood wainscoating above that, the bathroom was cozy, and it felt good to be warm again.

"Dusty," Mommy said, "I'm sorry I yelled at you. You *scared* me. I thought you might be hurt, and I was afraid. Do you understand?"

I nodded as I toed the braided oval rug on the floor.

"Good." She kissed me on the cheek and took my hand. "This is an important day, Dusty. It's Easter. We're going to church because Jesus is alive!"

The following weeks and months all run together in my

memory, but by the time I was four, I was beginning to feel the frustrations of a little boy with older sisters. Although I had no little brother to play with, I did have plenty of toys. Dad made me a hobby horse that I rode by the hour, and because my dad was the "King of the Cowboys," I had unusual Western toys, hobby horses, and wagons that said *Roy Rogers* on the side. My favorites were the army men—I had a ton of them—but one kind of toy set my teeth on edge. I hated dolls.

Cheryl and Linda, about eight and 10 years old, were forever playing with dolls. Daddy and Grampy had even built them a playhouse out by the pond, where they primped and fussed over their "babies" and gave them all their attention. I felt left out. The girls even hit me with their dolls, and one day I decided to get even. While the girls were at school, I went out to their playhouse, took all their dolls and "strung 'em up" by their necks.

When the girls came home, they screamed and cried, "Daddy! Daddy! Dusty's gone and hung all of our dolls!"

Daddy went out to investigate, and it seemed like a good idea for me to hide. Dad must have taken the stairs two at a time, because I never made it under the bed, which was my favorite hiding place. Dad caught me and blistered my bottom.

"Dusty, you can't go around hanging your sisters' dolls like that," he said afterwards as he cuddled me on his lap.

"Daddy," I cried, "we don't have any boys around here. We got nothin' but *girls* and dolls around here."

"Well, Dusty," he said, "maybe we'll have a boy some day. Maybe we will."

Not too long after that, Mommy and Daddy told us some exciting news—news that I couldn't really understand, but I was happy about it, just the same. We were going to have a baby.

Robin Elizabeth was special. She came into our lives like a little shining star, and she changed us all. Not only did she change us; she changed the lives of thousands of people because of her specialness.

That this new baby was to be the only natural child between my parents was plenty of reason to say she was special. But there was more to it than that. Mom was 37 when Robin was born, and I could tell that everyone was concerned about her and hoping everything would be all right.

Mom did have some trouble with her pregnancy. Not long after she realized she was pregnant, she came down with a mild case of German measles. Medical science had not yet realized the threat that German measles poses for unborn children, and since Mom didn't feel very sick, she had no idea what her illness could mean for our baby. As the months went on, Mom spent a lot of time in bed to avoid a miscarriage.

"We have to keep Mommy safe and well," Daddy explained, "so our baby will be healthy."

Finally, after what had seemed like forever to my five-year-old mind, Mommy went to the hospital, and on August 26, 1950, Robin was born. I don't even remember being disappointed that she wasn't a brother.

Virginia Peck was still our nanny, although we never called her that. A real stickler for clean clothes, shiny faces and freshly combed hair, she made us all scrub up special the day Mom and Robin came home.

Cheryl and Linda and I went out to the carport to wait. They didn't come and they didn't come, and I felt antsy. I got to squirming and teasing, and finally Virginia pulled us back into the house. We had to sit in the house and wait, since we didn't know what time Dad would be bringing them. I kept going to the window to look out.

Finally they came. It seemed like Mom had been gone a long time, and I was glad she was home, but I couldn't take my eyes off the tiny bundle she was holding. Cheryl and Linda thought of Robin as just another baby doll. They oohed and aahed and made funny noises, and they begged to hold her.

I just stood there, staring. I'd never seen a real baby before. She was pale—so white, so small. She *did* look like a little doll, a little Kewpie doll with blue almond-shaped eyes and little pixie ears. Then she moved! I touched her little hands. They were so tiny! Then they let me hold her, and although I hated dolls, I knew Robin was real. She belonged to us, and as far as I was concerned, we had it made.

I didn't know Robin was a Down's Syndrome baby. Not a lot was known about Down's Syndrome in those days.

Although recognized for centuries, there seemed to be no explanation of its cause. At that time it was called "mongolism,"and it was given that name because of the slanted eyes that are characteristic of a Down's baby. There were other problems, too. A thicker tongue than most people have. A weak cry. Poor muscle tone. A heart murmur. Developmental disabilities. Mental retardation.

But the day Mom brought her home, I knew none of this. I only knew she was our little baby. After Mom laid Robin in her little rattan bassinet, she told us she wanted to talk to us. She wanted to explain that Robin was different from other babies, and that she had some problems that kept her from being strong.

"Come here, Dusty and Cheryl. Linda Lou, sit here next to me," she said as she patted the sofa cushion. "I want to talk to you about our little Robin Elizabeth."

We cuddled up against Mom. It was good to have her home again, and though I wanted to go over and peek in at the new baby, I sat there and listened.

"Robin is a very special baby," Mom began. "She's not very strong, and she's going to be slower than other babies are. It will take her longer to drink her bottles, and she might not smile or talk as soon as other babies do. It may be a long time before she walks, and she'll never be able to do many of the things that you children can do. We have to take care of Robin just as though she were a delicate little flower, and you must help your daddy and me always to protect her. Do you understand?"

We couldn't fully understand, of course. I don't think anyone ever really understands immediately what it means to have a fragile baby, highly susceptible to illness, unable to develop in healthy, normal ways. What it means to watch the baby struggle to do things most babies do easily. What it means to know that, although the natural order of

27

things is for children to outlive their parents, this child may never reach adulthood. What it means to make a commitment to love and cherish and care for that child in the face of such odds. What it means to find value and purpose in pain. What it means to be enriched by the compassion and the understanding that can be gained by such an experience.

No, we didn't understand. Even the doctors didn't understand. In those days there was little tolerance for the mentally retarded and for people with special needs. Franklin D. Roosevelt's courage in the face of his challenge with polio and Helen Keller's triumph over blindness and deafness had broken down some of the walls fear and ignorance had built. But for the most part, even the doctors failed to see the human worth and value in a person who did not appear to be "normal."

Although some doctors encouraged Mom and Dad to take Robin home and love her, most of them advised my parents to place her in an institution and get on with their lives.

But my parents' lives had always included concern for sick and injured children. They were convinced God had sent Robin to us for a special reason, and that they had no right to cast her away. For whatever reason, the sovereign Lord of life had chosen us to be Robin's family, and her family we would be.

When Robin was eight months old we moved. Southern California winters are not especially rainy, but Los Angeles is a major seaport, and the ocean dampness settles in after about four in the afternoon. As you get closer to the sea, overcast days become more common. Further inland the days are sunnier and warmer, and Mom wanted Robin to have more sunshine. We moved to Encino, situated in the San Fernando Valley.

Like the Hollywood Hills house, the Encino house was an older, 10-room stucco Spanish-style ranch home built on four acres. Dad called it the Double R Bar Ranch.

The main house was huge. There was a big living room and a large kitchen with a table large enough for all of us. The master bedroom was at the right end of the house, and off to the left of the kitchen was the children's wing with a bedroom for each of us. In back, Dad's big den ran the length of the house.

Giant oak trees grew right up through the middle of the patio, and one of them was so old the Encino Chamber of Commerce saw fit to declare it a monument. Near the swimming pool was a little snack bar and two cabanas for dressing. At the end of the drive you could see the barn.

Having grown up on a farm in Duck Run, Ohio, Dad never lost his love for growing things and for animals. He made sure we had horses and dogs, ducks, chickens and geese, peacocks and guinea hens. We also had a large vegetable garden and a fruit orchard.

Robin seemed to thrive on the ranch. She learned to stand, and she enjoyed the animals. She liked to pet them, and our dog Lana became her favorite. Lana loved Robin, too, and was protective of her, following her around whenever we took her outside. But though Robin seemed to be happy on the ranch, she was highly sensitive to any kind of stimulation. She reacted nervously to any distraction, jerking and crying when she was startled.

Mom and Dad agreed with Cau-Cau, Robin's special round-the-clock nurse, that our baby needed a place of peace and quiet where distractions could be controlled, but they could not agree to sending Robin away from our family setting. They wanted her to remain part of our family as much as possible, to join us in her high chair at the table for meals and round-table prayers and to

29

sit with us during our family devotions.

Dad decided the answer was separate quarters, so he and Grampy Slye built a special little two-room house for Robin and Cau-Cau. Robin's room and bathroom was blue, and Mom put up white organdy curtains. The little house was a godsend, because it enabled us to keep Robin with us without disrupting normal family life and without sacrificing her special needs.

When Robin was a year old, she had a slight case of polio, but the rest of us were in no danger because she was always isolated from us when she was ill. She came through her illness with further physical damage: she could no longer stand, and she was considerably weaker.

We played with her when she was feeling okay, but my folks were concerned about our upsetting her. Because of her weak heart, we had to be careful not to overstimulate her. We were never allowed to be around her when she was sick or fretful.

When we did play together, I'd crawl under her bed and we would play peek-a-boo. She would smile and grin, and Mom was thrilled when she laughed. Robin had a sweet smile. Cheryl used to hold her and let her pound on the piano. Robin loved music and responded to it, and for Christmas Dad bought her a little toy piano of her own. Again, she responded with laughter—an indication that her mental retardation was not as severe as the doctors had originally expected.

One day we discovered something new; something that made Robin laugh and gave all of us hours of delight. Some people from the Encino Chamber of Commerce had come out to look at our old oak tree. It was covered with ivy that had been there for years, and they wanted us to take the ivy off because they were afraid it would eventually damage the tree. We cut the ivy down, and behind it, we found a nest of squirrels, we hadn't known were there.

"Oh, look at the babies!" Linda cried. Shorter than Cheryl, eight-year-old Linda had a little turned-up nose and fair skin. Her blond-brown hair was usually in braids, although sometimes she wore Shirley Temple curls. Tenderhearted, she worried about the baby squirrels, and when their mother didn't return for them, she asked Daddy how to take care of them.

Daddy fixed us a spot in the little cupboard just inside our back door. Then he found an eyedropper and showed us how to give the babies milk. A couple of them died, and Linda was heartbroken. She cried and cried. Finally, she stopped, found a shoe box and carefully lined it with soft cloth.

"Come on, Dusty," she said. "It's time for the funeral." We went out to the yard and dug a little hole in the flower bed, and Linda gently set the box inside. She covered it with dirt and put a little bouquet of geraniums on top. We stood there for a few minutes, and we prayed over the grave.

We didn't understand why these little creatures had died. Why they were too weak to survive. Why the mother hadn't returned to care for them. Why they had to suffer. All we knew was, they had mattered to us.

Two of the squirrels did survive. They graduated from the eye dropper to a toy baby bottle, and soon they were able to bite holes in the nipples. They were roly-poly little fur balls, and Robin laughed with delight whenever we showed them to her. She'd reach out to pet them, giggling when her hand touched the softness of their fur.

Mom and Dad were working themselves into exhaustion by this time. Robin's medical bills were astronomical, and Mom had lost nearly a year's income during her pregnancy and recovery from Robin's birth. Even if she had

31

been well enough to work, pregnant movie stars were taboo in Hollywood.

Now, she had no choice. She and Dad were up at 4:30 or 5:00 every morning, and often they didn't return home until after 8:00 at night. Looking back, I don't know how Mom kept up the pace. She managed to spend lots of time with Cheryl and Linda and me on the weekends, and she visited little Robin every night when she came home from the set.

It must have meant a lot to her that our three sets of grandparents were always available to us. It gave me a sense of security and continuity, too, because when I wasn't playing with Robin, I could visit them for a day or two while the girls were at school.

One day Grampy and I surprised my dad by showing up on the set. Grampy kicked the dirt around a bit with the toe of his boot and acted kind of uncomfortable.

"Pop, what's wrong?" Dad asked.

"Aw, son," Grampy finally said, "to put it bluntly, I'm tired of shovelin' chicken doo. I've about had it with that chicken ranch."

Dad was surprised. "Why, Pop! I thought you *liked* the chickens. That's why we bought the ranch." Grampy just toed the ground, and Dad shook his head. "Okay, Pop!" Dad grinned. "We'll sell it. What *do* you want to do?"

"Well, Leonard, I'd like to keep the place and sell all the chickens. I can still have a garden."

So Dad and Grampy sold the chicken ranch. Grampy and Mammy moved to the smaller place in Van Nuys, and the girls and I often went over. There was a little cottage in back of the main house, where we liked to sleep overnight.

When I was in high school Grampy suffered a stroke that left him helpless. Mammy died of a heart attack not

Mom, Robin and I enjoying our Encino, California backyard.

Dad and I feeding one of the baby squirrels we discovered in our tree.

long after that, so Grampy spent his final years in a convalescent hospital. Except when Dad was on the road, he visited Grampy every day for the last 10 years of his life.

But all of this lay ahead, and in the meantime, I felt lucky to have three sets of grandparents I enjoyed so much. Mom and Dad made sure we kept in touch with all of them.

After my natural mother died, we remained close to her parents. Like us, they lived in the San Fernando Valley. Grandpa Wilkins was tall—nearly 6'4"—with slightly rounded shoulders and bushy hair. I guess I got my height from him, because I'm about the same height, and like him, I walk like an old bear. He owned his own nursery; he could grow anything.

Grandma Wilkins was the typical grandmother—kind of pudgy and soft and easy to cuddle against. She fed us all the things we weren't supposed to eat—root beer floats, tapioca pudding, ice cream and apple pie. In fact, my first sentence was, "Apple pie all gone!"

One time she made a big batch of tapioca pudding and some pancake batter because she knew I was coming. Both bowls were sitting on the counter, and when she left the room, I snatched what I thought was the pudding and ate it. I figured I'd have dessert first because there was always room for pancakes. When Grandma came back into the kitchen to make the pancakes, I'd eaten all the batter!

Dale's parents lived in Texas, where she was born. Her real name was Frances Octavia Smith, and her mom's name was Betty Sue. She was short with strong facial features and a personality to match. She loved boys, and of course, she'd raised my stepbrother, Tom. I thought she was terrific.

My grandfather Smith looked like a southern plantation owner. He had a stern, strong nose and beautiful white wavy hair. Although he had kind of a poker face because he liked to gamble a bit, you always knew where you stood with him.

Even though we didn't see them as often as we saw our other grandparents, they always seemed close. It was reassuring to know they loved us and would be there for us, especially when times were tough.

Times must have been tough for Mom and Dad. Robin was weakening. Although they had accepted Robin's condition and realized she would probably not live very many years, they never gave up hope. They continued to look for new ways to make her comfortable and to give her as normal a life as possible.

Mom had heard about a specialist in San Francisco who worked with Down's Syndrome babies. She decided to have him look at our baby. Linda and Cheryl were in school, so Mom and Dad left Virginia in charge of them while they took Robin and me to San Francisco.

We went on the train. I had the berth above Robin, and Dad had the berth above Mom. In San Francisco we stayed at the Fairmont Hotel, and Dad's friend, Mel Williams took charge of me while Mom and Dad and Robin visited the doctor. We went for a ride on the cable cars, then we took the harbor cruise out to Alcatraz. I got seasick.

Robin didn't handle the trip very well. The city noises frightened her and by nightfall she was overstimulated. She cried most of the night. The trip home was hard because the baby was sick, and Mom and Dad were sad. The doctor had told them there was nothing he could do for Robin, except to give her some extra vitamins.

Summer came and went, and before I knew it Mommy said it was time for me to start kindergarten. I didn't want to go. It was more fun to stay home and play peek-a-boo with Robin. The school was only a few blocks away, and most of the time we walked. On the days Mom left late for the set, she drove the girls and me to school.

We didn't have regular classrooms; they were more like bungalows or trailers. There was an airspace underneath them, and we had to climb up steps to go in. My room was big. It had a big chalkboard and long tables with little chairs. The floor was masonite, and I remember one of the other boys sliding on it.

I didn't like school. I wanted to be outside, or home with our baby. The other kids didn't want to play with me. I didn't understand why. One day we were building something out of blocks and the other kids were teasing me. I don't recall what they were teasing me about, but I remember feeling badly about it. I moved away from them and began building a castle of my own. One of the boys got up and threw a block at my castle and knocked it down. I jumped up and went after him with a block, and the teacher sent me to the office. Virginia had to come to the school and take me home. I was glad.

In April Mom made a trip to Texas to visit her parents. While she was there, she stopped off in Dallas to visit Hope Cottage, where Dad had found Cheryl. Cheryl had been feeling anxious about being adopted, and she wanted to know about her real mother.

Mom talked to the advisors at the Cottage, and they urged her to delay the search until Cheryl was old enough to handle possible rejection. Mom followed their advice, but eventually she was able to help Cheryl locate her natural mother. Cheryl had graduated from high school by the time that happened, and it turned out to be a positive experience.

Meanwhile, at Hope Cottage, Mom was mesmerized by the big dark eyes of a beautiful little Indian baby, who

36

was part Choctaw like Dad. She cuddled the baby and left the Cottage praying that God would send just the right family for the child who reminded her of a happy little fawn.

I was glad when summer came. I could swim like a fish, and I enjoyed the pool. Robin loved the water. Dad said she looked like an angel and swam like a frog! She kicked and splashed and laughed. I loved the way she laughed.

But one day Cheryl said she didn't feel good. My throat hurt and I had a headache, too. It was hard to swallow, impossible to chew, and soon we began to resemble our nest full of greedy chipmunks. The doctor confirmed Mom's suspicions: it was mumps. He suggested ice packs to ease the pain. Sometimes I put mine on my swollen neck, and sometimes I plopped it on my head.

But worse than being sick was the concern we had for Robin, and though we kept her isolated in her little house, she, too, came down with the mumps on a Wednesday, about a week before her second birthday. Linda and Cheryl and I recovered with no problem, but our baby was dangerously sick.

The infection went to Robin's brain, and by Saturday night she had been screaming in pain for nearly a week. Her temperature was over 108°. The doctor told Mom Robin had mumps encephalitis. If she recovered, she would suffer severe brain damage.

Mom fixed us our breakfast on Sunday morning, but we weren't very hungry. Suddenly everything was quiet. Robin had stopped screaming and lapsed into unconciousness. By late afternoon it was as though a cannon had exploded, shocking the world into silence. Even the birds were mute.

Time seemed to stand still, and everything ground to a halt. The lights in the house seemed dimmer, darker, somehow, and nobody spoke. I kept going to the window and looking out the blinds.

I tried to ask what was happening, but nobody would answer. The only sound I could hear was an occasional howl from Lana, who had placed herself outside the door of Robin's little house. I went over to the window again and looked out. Mom and Dad were in the carport crying. They just stood there holding each other and cried for what seemed like hours to me.

Viriginia was crying too when she came to me. She hugged me gently and told me that my baby sister had "passed away." I tried to go outside, but the entry was closed and the lights were out. Cheryl and Linda were crying, Virginia was crying and Mom and Dad were crying. Everywhere I went, I got no answers. There were only tears.

Mom and Dad sent the girls and me to stay with Mammy and Grampy for several days, and we didn't go to the funeral. Robin was buried on her second birthday, but for weeks I kept going to the nursery door and peeking in. I kept thinking she would come back. Mom told me that Robin had gone to heaven to be with Jesus, and that she was happy there and would never have any more pain. I was glad about that, but I missed our baby.

Mom and Dad were devastated. Mom looked tired and *different,* somehow. I don't know when I realized the reason she looked so different. That summer, her hair had turned completely white.

Sometimes when a great grief enters your life, there seems to be no way of redeeming the pain. But my mom is an amazing woman, and she somehow sensed that God would sanctify her sadness in the sharing of it. She sat down and wrote a little book about Robin and called it *Angel Unaware.*

As a way of helping others, she designated all of the royalties to go to the National Association for Retarded Children. Today that book is in its twenty-eighth printing. It has comforted thousands of families with children like Robin, and it has challenged the world to be compassionate.

Dad, too, had changed. After Robin's death he began to use Christian music in his shows, and he told the children in his audiences that it isn't sissy stuff to trust God and go to Sunday School. Even today we hear testimonies about young boys who gave their lives to Christ because Roy Rogers said it was important.

So Robin did touch our lives. She showed us the value of human life, revealed to us that pain can be redeemed, and taught us the meaning of grace.

A reluctant first handshake with the new kid, Sandy.

It didn't take Sandy and me too long to become inseparable.

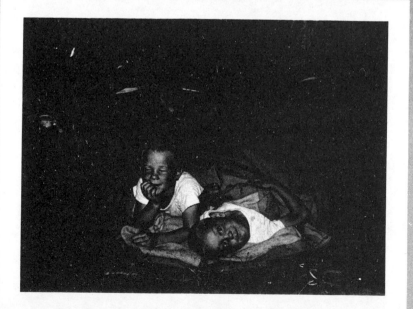

three

In the weeks that followed Robin's funeral my parents found themselves back on the personal appearance circuit. Just a month after Robin died, they were scheduled to appear at Madison Square Garden in New York. The show, with more than 40 performances in less than 30 days, was expected to play to more than 700,000 people.

As they had done many times before and would do many times again, Mom and Dad set aside their personal feelings, their stresses, their grief. "The show must go on" is a cliche, but that doesn't alter the fact that it is also an expectation. It doesn't matter if you're sick. No one cares if you have problems at home.

Fans don't understand the long hours, the hard work, the sore muscles, and the fatigue that make you tired clear down into tomorrow. All they see is excitement and glitter and dazzle. They wonder about box office receipts and fan letters, newspaper reviews, fancy clothes and parties—but fans cannot begin to fathom the mental, physical and emotional price a performer must pay for popularity.

Whatever motivates a performer, whether it's the need for recognition or monetary reward or some other aim, there's a price to pay. For my parents the price was relinquishing their right to privacy, to rest during illness, to take time to grieve. Many times they fought off headaches, sore throats, fevers and flu symptoms to fulfill their obligations to their fans.

"After all," Dad would say, "these people have made me what I am. I owe them something. If it weren't for them, I wouldn't be doing what I love to do."

What they loved to do was to perform, but they also loved to be with us. In spite of long separations while they were on the road, they spent quality time with us when they could. During the summers we were together almost every day because we traveled with them.

But the summer Robin died, we stayed home. Mom and Dad phoned us every night while they were away, and just before they were to return home, they called with a special announcement.

"Dusty," Mom said, "we'll be home in time for your birthday. I'll bake you a special cake. What do you want for your birthday dinner?"

"Fried chicken and mashed potatoes! And a chocolate cake with chocolate frosting and jelly beans on top!" Mom couldn't have been surprised. I always asked for that.

"Sounds good, Honey," she told me. "And guess what? We're going to bring you a *real* surprise. We're bringing you a new baby sister! Her name is Mary Little Doe, and we're going to call her Dodie!"

After Robin's death, Mom remembered the little Indian baby she had seen at Hope Cottage in April. Hoping

42

she would still be there, they had stopped in Dallas on their way to the East Coast, and they asked about the baby.

At first the director of the Cottage discouraged them because the law required Indian children to be adopted by Indian parents. But when Dad reminded the Board of Directors that he was part Choctaw, the problem was settled. Mary Little Doe would be ours. I missed Robin so much that the idea of a new baby sister sounded good to me.

On my sixth birthday, Virginia got the three of us scrubbed and ready to meet the airplane. She made us take baths and wash behind our ears and brush our teeth.

"Now you guys got to look real sharp because we're taking you to meet your new baby sister."

It was bad enough having to get all cleaned up, and what little excitement I had left was dampened considerably when I realized Virginia was going to make me wear a suit. I had a new wind-up piggy bank, and to pacify me, she let me take it with me in the car.

When we got to the airport, the reporters were already waiting. My stepbrother, Tom, and his wife Barbara were there, too. Then I saw Mom and Dad get off the airplane. Mommy was carrying our new baby.

Dodie was tiny, and she was wearing Robin's little pink coat and hat. "Why does she have such a dark suntan?" I asked.

"Because Dodie is part Indian," Virginia explained. I thought the baby was pretty.

Suddenly I realized something was terribly wrong. There was someone else with Mommy and Daddy and Dodie. He was a little boy, smaller than me, wearing a suit and a cap. Worst of all, he was holding *my* daddy's hand.

Just before the security people permitted us to go to

43

the airplane steps, Virginia put my piggy bank in my hand.

"Now you give this to your new *brother*," Virginia was saying, "and you put your arms around him and hug him and kiss him so he knows you like him."

The whole idea sounded terrible. "Well," I said soberly, "if I have to give him this pig, that's *all* he's getting!"

We walked to the airplane, and when I got close enough, Mom said, "Dusty, we brought you a surprise. This is your new brother, Sandy!" Today, Mom says they made a mistake in not preparing me in advance for my new brother. It was always hard for me to adjust to new people, but they didn't realize I would perceive this little tyke as a threat.

Sandy stepped forward and reached out his hand to me. "Howdy, pardner," he said.

I ignored him. But I also kept my eyes on him to make sure he didn't get into my back pocket or something. The photographers were taking pictures like crazy, and Dodie and Sandy were getting all kinds of attention. To make matters worse, that boy was calling *my* parents *Mommy* and *Daddy*.

This is just terrible, I decided. *Just terrible.*

I didn't say a word all the way home. But no one noticed. All the grown-ups were anxious to hear about how Mom and Dad found *him*.

"After the show at Madison Square Garden," Mom said, "we had to play three other cities on our way back to California: Cincinnati, Ohio; Muncie, Indiana; and Owensboro, Kentucky. From Kentucky we were going to stop in Dallas to pick up our new little Indian baby." She snuggled closer to the baby.

"When we got into Cincinnati there was a stack of mail," Dad interrupted. "I was born in Cincinnati, Dusty.

44

Did you know that? Anyway, I went through the mail, and there was a wire from a woman who ran a home for disadvantaged children in Covington, Kentucky. That's just across the river from Cincinnati. She wanted me to call her."

"Daddy's always a soft touch for kids in trouble," Linda noted.

"Uh huh," Mom nodded, "and our little Robin made you even more sensitive, didn't she, Daddy?"

Dad just fingered the leather of the upholstery. Compliments make him bashful.

"The woman told me she had a little girl in a wheelchair who really wanted to see me, but they didn't have tickets to the show. I told her to meet our PR man backstage. Then I thought about Dusty and all these girls! I asked the lady if she had a little boy about five or six years old that we could bring home for you Dusty."

I didn't answer. Daddy still had his arm around the new kid.

"She started to say no, at first, didn't she, Daddy?" Mommy asked.

Dad nodded. "But then she said, 'Yes, we do have one, Mr. Rogers, but I don't think you'd be interested in him. He's got a few problems.' I told her to bring him along." Dad gave the boy another squeeze. I turned and stared out the window.

"The night of the show they didn't arrive until Daddy was already on stage," Mom said. "After the first number, he noticed the woman with the little girl in the wheelchair, and beside her was *this* tiny little fellow wearing a yellow corduroy suit and one of those short billed caps. How old are you, Sandy?"

"Five."

"That's right!" said Mom.

45

I thought he didn't look any bigger than a three-year-old.

"When Sandy saw Daddy," Mom continued, "his whole face lit up. He stepped forward with his hand out. What did you say to Daddy, Honey?"

"Howdy, pardner!" Sandy repeated as Dad hugged him again.

Dad has a thing about handshakes. He always says, "If you're going to shake hands, shake hands like you mean it!" That little fella must have meant it, because Dad had simply melted. Although Mom usually does most of the talking, Dad finished the story as Sandy dozed against his chest.

The boy's name was bigger than he was—Harry John David Hardy—and he was in terrible shape. He'd been abandoned three times before he was eight months old. He'd either been dropped on his face or beaten, and he had an unrepaired broken nose. He could hardly breathe, and he had obvious physical problems.

Dad took the lady's telephone number, and after the show he and Mom talked for hours. They discussed what it would mean to take in another handicapped child. There was no doubt he was handicapped, and no denying the potential problems in adopting a child who had so obviously been abused.

Finally my dad said, "Anybody can take in a perfect child. What happens to a little guy like this?"

"Within 24 hours we had all the papers signed," Mom added, "and we whisked this little fellow out of Kentucky. Daddy decided he needed a nickname, so we called him Sandy."

"I've got one boy named Dusty and one named Sandy," Dad teased. "If we ever get another one, we'll have to call him Filthy!"

"Poor little guy," Mom mused. "The night we left, we were on a bus with the cast of the show. He'd eaten so much dinner, he lost it all. I felt so sorry for him. We stopped at a hotel and had a roll away bed put in our room for Sandy."

"He was scared to death," Dad added. "All night long he kept getting up and coming over to our bed to see if we were still there."

"Then we went on to Dallas to pick up Dodie at the Cottage. While we were in the office talking to the matron, Sandy kept peeking around the door to make sure we didn't leave him."

But none of this changed my mind about the new kid. I didn't like him. When we got home, Mommy dropped another bomb on me. Sandy was going to sleep in *my* room. All night long he tossed and turned, crying out in his sleep. The next morning I hid as many of my toys as I could before I left for school.

"What are you doing, Dusty?" Mom asked.

"I'm hiding my toys, case that new guy tries to make off with any of 'em. Is he going to stay long?"

She knelt down beside me. "Sandy is your new brother, Dusty," she said firmly, emphasizing his name. "He's going to live with us from now on, and he's going to share your room with you. He doesn't want to take your toys. He wants to be your friend."

I wasn't so sure about that, but within a day or two, I decided Sandy was all right. Probably to "seal the deal," Dad took Sandy and me on a fishing trip up near Marysville in northern California. Dad's favorite fishing hole was there. We took camping gear—sleeping bags and whatnot—but no food because Dad likes to "live off the land."

We had a great time. We used multiple lines with four

hooks on each line, and we put cheese balls on the hooks. Dad was so busy baiting the hooks, I don't know if he ever had time to fish, but Sandy and I pulled in 136 bluegill in about two hours one day. What we didn't eat or throw back, we gave away to other people camping in the area.

Dad shot rabbits and showed us how to clean them by running a knife right up the middle. Then he'd have us pull out the innards so we'd know how. Since we didn't take any skillets with us, we made an open fire and cooked them over the spit. He showed us how to clean and bone fish, and how to check rabbits for warbles, which are the larva of the warble fly. When those things get in a rabbit, it's not fit to eat.

Dad had taken me hunting and fishing many times, and he'd started me shooting about a year before, but to Sandy all of this was new. He dove into it headfirst.

Sandy wasn't the least bit squeamish about it. I think his stomach was made of cast iron, but it must have had a hole in it somewhere, because we couldn't seem to fill him up! Anyway, Dad showed us how to catch frogs and cut their legs off. We'd put them on the end of a stick and hold them over the fire. Then we'd roast them until the meat turned white. To this day I love to eat frog legs.

At night we crawled into our sleeping bags and looked up into the sky. It was clear, and we could see thousands of stars. Chirping crickets sang us lullabies as we dozed off to sleep. It felt good to be out-of-doors with my dad and my brother, and even though the mosquitoes about ate us alive, that trip was worth every moment. By the time it was over, Sandy was my best friend.

When we got home, Mom took Sandy and Dodie to the doctor for checkups. Although Dodie was just fine, Sandy was not. His head was enlarged, his bones were soft and pliable, and he had curvature of the spine, all due to rickets and malnutrition. An EEG (electroencephalogram), which tests brainwaves, revealed a slight abnormality.

His muscle tone was terrible. Because his face had been smashed, he had almost no bridge to his nose. He needed reconstructive surgery, and he needed to have his tonsils removed. He was hospitalized for the necessary surgery, and although he came back from the hospital looking battered and bruised, he was happy to be home.

In the days that followed Sandy's surgery, we began to realize how terribly abused he must have been at the care facility. He told us he'd been hit with a baseball bat one day when he dropped a baby bottle. As tiny as he was, he had been responsible for changing baby diapers and for feeding other children, as well as caring for the girl in the wheelchair. Whenever he was "bad," they made him sleep in a chair out on the porch. A couple of times, he said, he woke up with snow all over him.

Sandy spent a lot of time crying that first year. Little things reminded him of his early experiences, and he often burst into tears. He had frequent nightmares and dreams that he was falling. One night, terrified, he woke me up.

"Dusty!" he hissed as he shook me awake. "Dusty! Wake up! There's someone in this room."

"What do you mean there's somebody in the room, Sandy? There's nobody here."

"Right over there. Look!"

All I could see was a shirt hanging in the closet. "Sandy," I said, "it's just a shirt." But Sandy would see things that weren't there, like shadows on curtains. Even though Mom would get up and rock him in the rocking chair, soothing him and calming him down, he was plagued with nightmares all during his growing-up years.

If the nightmares affected his sleep, they certainly had no ill effect on his appetite. Sandy was *always* hungry. I

49

think sometimes when people have known the kind of malnutrition and deprivation Sandy had experienced, food becomes a kind of security for them. Whatever the reason, Sandy approached every meal as if it were his first and last for all time.

Most people would take a cereal bowl for breakfast, but not Sandy. He'd take the largest mixing bowl in the kitchen, pour a whole box of cereal in it, drown it in a half-gallon of milk and sit there shoveling in the whole thing.

Once Sandy recovered from his surgery and was stronger, Mom started him in school. By this time Cheryl and Linda were in junior high school. One day Mom couldn't drive us to school because she was getting ready to make a personal appearance. When she was dressed in her Western outfit with the fringe and her leather boots and her cowgirl hat, she kissed us at the door and waved us on.

Suddenly one of us got a great idea—*one* of us did.

"Hey, Sandy, look! The mailman's only a couple of houses ahead of us!"

"Yeah. So what?"

"Wouldn't it be funny if we went along behind him and switched everybody's mail?"

Sandy didn't need much persuasion because he usually went along with whatever I suggested. He wanted so much to belong and to fit that he never really thought about the consequences—not that I was giving them much thought, either.

We'd switched the mail at several houses before we heard a car coming up behind us. The next thing I knew, the brakes squealed. I turned around just in time to see Mom flying out of the car.

She took her belt off and ran toward us, yelling like a Comanche. Sandy and I started yelling and crying before she got within 10 feet of us, and she was hollering that she was going to whip the daylights out of us. She paddled us all the way up the block, missing three swats out of four, and made us put all the mail back where it belonged along the way.

It must have been a sight: this cowgirl chasing two little boys up the street with a belt; letters dropping everywhere; the car sitting in the middle of the road with the motor running and the door wide open. But Mom believed in swift discipline, and it wouldn't be the last time she laid into Sandy and me. The two of us were about to give her a real run for her money.

Although there was a difference of only eight months in our ages, at the age of six, Sandy looked several years younger than me. I stood head and shoulders above him, and because I'd had the advantage of good nutrition and lots of time outdoors, I was stronger and healthier. Sandy also lacked the kind of coordination he needed to ride well, to hit a target, and to play many of the games boys like to play, so I tended to outshine him in those areas.

I don't remember feeling sorry for Sandy, but Robin had taught me so much about being gentle and compassionate that I simply assumed a protective attitude toward my brother. He had become my best buddy, and anybody who picked on him at school had to answer to me.

The summer after Sandy came to live with us, we discovered something he could always do better than me, and it had to do with that cast-iron stomach of his. Dad had purchased an old surplus PT boat and converted it to a recreational fishing boat, complete with diving rigs, and he named it *The Flamba*.

The boat was berthed at Wilmington Harbor, and sometimes on weekends the whole family would pack up and head for the beach. The boat could sleep 14, so the girls sometimes brought their friends and we'd head out to sea. The first time out, Sandy and I were beside ourselves with excitement.

"You fellas are in for a real treat," Dad told us. "Out on the ocean you can catch fish without a pole and without a net!"

I was doubtful. By this time I'd been fishing a lot, and I couldn't see how it could be done. "How do you do that?" I asked.

"You'll see, Dusty," Dad chuckled. "There are flying fish in the ocean. During the night they'll just leap up on the deck! All we have to do is clean 'em and fry 'em up for breakfast."

Sandy and I were all eyes as we climbed aboard. The air was fresh, and we could smell the salt. The sun beat down on us and warmed our faces, but the ocean breeze kept us from feeling too hot. Soon the motor started up, and we headed toward the breakwater.

The boat bounced along and Sandy was whooping and hollering and having the time of his life. I stood next to a rail watching the horizon go up and down, up and down and it wasn't very long before I thought my stomach was going to turn inside out.

"You okay, Honey?" Mom asked.

"Uh uh," I groaned. "I feel just awf—."

The next thing I knew my stomach *had* turned inside out. I wanted, more than anything in the world, to die. There's no worse feeling than being seasick and knowing that there's no way off the boat for the next couple of days—which might as well be for eternity.

Mom gave me some soda crackers and tried to talk to me to get my mind off my misery. When things let up a bit, I wondered how ol' Sandy was doing. If his rough-and-tumble brother, who outshined him in every physical activity, couldn't take it, Sandy must be near death.

Just then Sandy came whooping down the deck with a sandwich in one hand and a paper cup in the other. "Hey, Dusty, your face is kinda green. You feeling bad? Daddy says you're seasick!" He grinned again. Every time we went out after that, he grinned and I threw up. I was probably the only one in the family who was glad when Dad sold *The Flamba*. I secretly celebrated when I heard she had sunk off a Florida reef some time later.

In the meantime, Sandy and I had become like fly and fly paper—and sometimes we got ourselves into sticky situations. Mom was both creative and swift in dealing with our antics. One day she caught us swiping pennies.

"Boys! Stealing is a crime. Do you understand?"

Sandy and I just stood there; we didn't say a word.

"Nothing to say for yourselves, huh? Well, when people steal, they go to jail, and they only get to eat bread and water!"

Sandy shifted from one foot to the other and shrugged.

"Okay, then. Now you boys have to go to jail for the whole day, and you have to subsist on bread and water!"

We didn't know what *subsist* meant, but we started crying anyway. Mom took Sandy by the hand and grabbed me by the ear, and she locked us inside the cabanas.

"Now you boys can stay here all day. *You are in jail!*"

Sandy and I kept hollering after she left. A few minutes later she came back with a hunk of dry bread and a little cup of water for each of us. Every 15 or 20 minutes or so, she came out to check on us. By the second hour, we weren't upset anymore at all.

Each time Mom came out, we were grinning, but we kept quiet. Finally it happened: Mom caught on. Linda's compassion had gotten the best of her, and she had been smuggling us cookies and milk!

(Clockwise from center) Cheryl, Dad, Mom and Linda wait for the amateur cameraman to make his adjustments.

four

As much as our folks tried to give us lives that paralleled those of other children, we were living a unique paradox. We knew few Hollywood stars, and yet our lives were touched by the men and women—and the animals—that worked with Mom and Dad in the movies, on television, and on the road shows. The razzle-dazzle of show business was very much a part of who we were, but I suppose none of us took it quite as seriously as Cheryl did.

Cheryl was a real "show biz kid," and she loved to go down to the set with Mom and Dad. She took very seriously her role as "the daughter of" Roy Rogers, King of the Cowboys. She had brown Shirley Temple curls and a round face with expressive eyes. She carried herself so regally that the rest of us all called her "Queenie." Cheryl retaliated by dubbing me "Prince."

But Queenie wasn't the only one who enjoyed being on

the set. Sandy and I loved it, and it was there that I learned to drink coffee. There was never anything for kids to drink on the set, so I would get half a cup of coffee, fill the rest up with half-and-half, then dunk donuts in it.

Sandy and I loved being on the sets because we liked to watch the stunts. We'd go home and try to imitate them, or sometimes we'd roll around on the set. One day Sandy rolled a rock onto my hand and pinched it a bit. I let out a shriek right in the middle of a big scene, and everyone came running. As soon as Mom and Dad knew I was all right, I was in deep trouble for messing up the scene. If I wanted to do stunts, Dad said, I had to do them at home. The set was *his* place to do them.

A couple of times Cheryl and I even played parts in the television series. I played the town brat, and I was always picking on Pat Brady. In one scene, I shot his hat off with a bow and arrow, and in another, I got him in the rear end with a sling shot.

We never thought of Pat as a "star." He was simply one of Dad's best friends, and he and his wife Fayetta were Dodie's godparents. Pat had bright red hair and a face like rubber. He could make the most wonderful faces. Although he was almost as shy as my dad, he was the biggest practical joker, always trying to sneak in funny things to get Dad's goat. He put smoke bombs under the hoods of the police escorts at the fairs and rodeos, or cherry bombs under their tires.

During the road shows Pat always tried to throw Dad's concentration off. Part of their act was target shooting. Pat tossed up a series of clay pigeons, and Dad shot them. A terrific marksman, Dad never missed.

One day Pat stuffed one of the pigeons with a pair of lady's nylons. Dad was blazing away when all of a sudden, BOOM! The nylons came floating down. It flustered Dad, but he didn't miss the next target. Another time Pat put a little parachute inside, and the kids in the audience went wild as it floated down.

Once Pat really succeeded at bewildering my dad. He had one of the pigeons made out of aluminum instead of clay, so when the bullet hit it, the pigeon would simply fall to the ground instead of shattering. Before that segment of the act, Pat announced to the audience, "This is Roy's 156th show, and not once has he missed!" The crowd hushed, Pat let the pigeon fly, Dad blasted away, and the target came down and hit the dirt.

The whole audience gasped and went, "Ahhhhh!"

Dad couldn't believe it! "But I never miss," he muttered, walking over to the pigeon. As soon as he picked it up he knew what had happened, so he dropped it. It clattered down the stage, and the kids realized it was a big put-on. Dad started chasing Pat around, and the kids really ate it up. They kept that in the act for awhile after that. Those days were great fun, and when Pat was killed in an auto accident some 20 years later, in the late seventies, we were all heartbroken.

But those hard times were ahead of us. These were the fifties, the early years when Dad did most of his own stunts. He was really upset when the studio bigwigs made him stop because they thought he'd become too valuable to the studio to risk his getting hurt. In later years he had a stunt double, although he continued to do some of his own horse mounts, some of the fighting, and all of the tricks with Trigger.

Together, Dad and Trigger were like a smooth-running machine. There never was a better matchup between a man and a horse. Trigger could run wild at a full gallop, and Dad always sat solid in the saddle. Dad did 88 pictures with him, and Trigger never fell in any of them. Dad was the only cowboy star to make all of his pictures with the same horse. One time they were going down a steep hill, and Trigger slipped. He knew if he rolled, Dad would fall off, so instead of rolling, which would have been better for him, Trigger slid his legs down and kept Dad safe on his back.

Trigger had real personality, and he liked to tease Dad a bit, especially when they were on stage. Trigger seemed to know that Dad couldn't discipline him in front of an audience. In the arena shows and rodeos, Dad had an act about the cowboy and his loyal horse. The announcer painted a word picture about the cowboy riding through outlaw-infested country, in danger of being shot at any time.

Dad galloped out on Trigger, and suddenly a shot rang out. Dad slumped in his saddle, but Trigger kept running. Then a second shot rang out. Trigger stumbled a bit, then started running again, this time limping because one of his legs was wounded. He limped along like that for 25 or 30 feet, getting weaker and weaker, and then he went down.

Dad rolled out of the saddle and lay along side of him. Someone played "Taps" and the lights went out briefly so Dad could get back on Trigger and they could take a bow. After they had been doing this act for a few weeks, Trigger got ornery, and he would try to get up so Dad couldn't get back on him in time.

Trigger started tensing at the last note of "Taps," and during rehearsal he would bound up and try to run away, leaving Dad in the arena. Dad disciplined him each time, but he knew the children would be upset if he had to do that during a show. Dad kept a firm grip on the saddle and the reins, and he'd throw his leg over the saddle just in time to pull up the reins and keep the horse in tow.

One night they had taken their fall, and Dad could feel all of Trigger's muscles tensing. He kept a firm grip on the saddle horn just in case, and sure enough, at the last note of "Taps" and just as the lights went off, Trigger took off like a skyrocket. Dad "pony-expressed" it out the side entrance, but it must have felt to him like he was flying along beside Trigger like a flag.

Near the grandstands, Trigger stopped suddenly and Dad hit the ground, hard enough to flip him clear up and over Trigger to the other side. Somehow Dad managed to pull himself back up into the saddle. Thinking it was a stunt, the audience roared with applause.

Backstage, Dad brushed himself off and looked around, furious. Spotting the little training whip he used for disciplining his horses, he grabbed it and headed for the horse. Suddenly Trigger started dancing the carioca! To Dad's amusement, his palomino went through his entire repertoire—every trick Dad had ever taught him, including playing dead! How could he whip Trigger after that?

Dad loved that horse as much as he loved any of us kids, I think. In fact, Mom used to tease him about his golden palomino, and once she wrote a tongue-in-cheek song with the mile-long title, "Don't Ever Fall in Love with a Cowboy (He'll Love His Horse the Best)." Ironically, the song was released just about the time they announced their engagement.

But Dad wasn't the only one who loved Trigger. The children of the nation loved him, too, and sometimes they would line up for blocks just to see his saddle! Once a man from Texas offered Dad $250,000 for Trigger. Before Dad could say no, his publicity agent started a rumor that Dad was thinking of selling Trigger.

Before long, Dad's mailbox was flooded with nickles and dimes and quarters—even some silver dollars—from children all over the country, pleading with Dad not to sell Trigger. Some of them were addressed simply, "To Roy and

Dad performing during his shooting act.

Dad and Trigger: There never was a better team.

Trigger." The thought of selling Trigger broke their hearts. It took weeks to trace down every letter and return the money. To reassure the children, Dad announced that Trigger was not going to be sold because he not only belonged to Roy Rogers, but also to all of the children of the world. Then he had thousands of certificates of honorary ownership printed. Every child who asked for one received printed proof of being an honorary shareholder in Trigger, the Smartest Horse in the Movies.

One Easter morning we got a call from the stables where Trigger and most of Dad's other horses were kept. Trigger had sired a colt, and the foal looked just like him. We all went out to the stable before church to look at him. The colt never got to be as big as Trigger, but he was smart. Dad hired a fantastic horse trainer, Glen Randall, to train the colt. He taught the animal about 20 different dances, and Dad did all of his dance sequences on him.

Trigger lived to be 33 years old—more than 100 years in human terms. His golden hair had grayed considerably, and he was gray around his eyes and ears. When Trigger died in 1965 Dad was so broken up he never told anyone about it, not even us, for more than a year.

Because Trigger was not a pet, Dad kept him and all of his entertainment horses on a separate ranch. By the time Trigger died, he wasn't making movies anymore, so no one ever questioned. Dad had Trigger mounted and he placed him in the Roy Rogers and Dale Evans Museum in Victorville, California. That way, he reasoned, people could always enjoy him. Dad gets his nose out of joint when he hears people say that Trigger is "stuffed."

"That just shows they don't understand," Dad says. "It makes it sound like he's an old rag doll."

Actually, the taxidermist takes the animal's measurements, then makes a mold out of Styrofoam. Over that they make a fiberglass frame. When the fiberglass hardens the Styrofoam is removed and the animal skin is stretched over the fiberglass.

Dad also had Trigger Jr. and Mom's horse, Buttermilk, mounted that way. Their dog Bullet, as well as many of Dad's hunting trophies, are all on permanent display at the museum.

When people ask, "Why in the world did you have them mounted?" Dad has a standard answer.

"People all over the world enjoyed Trigger so much, why stick him in the ground? Why not put him up where people can look at him and enjoy him? In fact, when I go, you can stick me up there with him!" Mom says not to get any ideas about her!

I'm not sure when Dad decided to build a museum, but it probably happened not too long after he visited a small Will Rogers Museum in Los Angeles. Dad had chosen "Rogers" for his stage name because of his admiration for the American humorist who lost his life in a tragic air crash in 1935. Will Rogers was probably Dad's all-time favorite entertainer. Dad was delighted with the memorabilia displayed at the Will Rogers Museum in Oklahoma, but he was disappointed that the museum in Los Angeles didn't have more items to reveal what Will Rogers' life was like.

Because Dad is committed to the principle that a star belongs to the fans who make him a star in the first place, he began to save everything that his fans might find interesting. Until he was able to build his museum, he kept it all in storage, including fan letters.

At one time he was receiving so much fan mail that all of his salary went to pay for postage, photos, and the salaries of the women he hired to help with the mail. Because Republic Pictures refused to help with the costs involved, Dad had to go on road shows in order to make a living!

Eventually he was receiving more than a million letters each year, and every one of them was answered.

Also included at the museum are samples, or at least photos, of most of the commercial products Dad and Mom endorsed through the years. A complete list would include more than 125 products made by 74 different manufacturers.

Because all of these items were aimed at children, Dad and Mom insisted that the quality be good. Each item had to be durable and safe. That's where we kids came in.

Every product was tested on us before it hit the public. Consequently, we had Roy Rogers beds, bedspreads, curtains, toothbrushes, Viewmasters, boots, sweaters, cookies, slipper socks, watches, clocks, raincoats, gloves and moccasins. There were Roy Rogers look-alike masks, suspenders, cameras, gun belts, scarves, tables, chairs, dishes, glasses, blankets, wagons and bootsters to fit over shoes for children who didn't have boots.

We had Roy Rogers rugs, wallets, holsters, shooting irons, ropes, binoculars, knives, hobby horses, tents, bunkhouses, flashlights, bow ties, hats, pants, socks, bookbags, shirts, blouses, skirts, sweat shirts, T-shirts and pajamas. There were even Roy Rogers milk glasses. They were specially marked, and if you drank a fourth of a glass, you were a tenderfoot. From there it went up through posse member, posse leader, then deputy, and finally a sheriff.

Dad said, "If these things can survive you guys, they'll work for everyone else." So, if we beat the stuff to death and it was still in good shape, it would go on the market. We wore out pants by sliding down rocks, and Mom would put patches on the bottoms, and we'd bang up our lunch pails something fierce.

I got so tired of wearing Roy Rogers stuff! But the real

kicker was that Roy Rogers lunch box. Everyone else had Zorro or Hop-A-Long Cassidy, and they would rib Sandy and me because we had "Roy Rogers." As if that weren't bad enough, Mom was never one to buy cookies or Twinkies or any of that good stuff. No, we had to have carrot sticks!

One time I complained about it, and she did send cookies. I couldn't believe it. They were *carrot* cookies, of all things! There it was again—the paradox of being the children of Roy Rogers and Dale Evans. No matter how many commercial products came our way, and in spite of the great success my parents knew, Mom and Dad never forgot the poverty they experienced during the Great Depression. So, they saved everything. Instead of wrapping our sandwiches in waxed paper, like every other mother did, Mom used the plastic wrapper the bread came in.

There I'd be, with all the other kids. They opened their Gene Autry lunch pails, and everything would be in there, all neat and tidy. I opened mine, and it looked like World War II all over again. Mom never let us peel our own hard-boiled eggs. She'd peel the egg, dump some salt in a bread wrapper and throw in the egg. Sometimes she'd even toss the sandwich in after it. She sliced up some apples and rolled them in the tinfoil she'd wrapped the roast in the night before.

Because there were so many of us, Mom never bought packaged lunch meat or cheese. Instead, she bought them in big 20-pound loaves or chunks, and sliced it herself. Sometimes the bologna would be an inch thick and the cheese would be paper thin. Other times both of them would be really thick on one side and tapered down to nothing on the other.

We always had to have milk, never Kool-Aid or lemon-

Dad with one weeks worth of fan mail.

(From left to right) Linda, Cheryl drinking
milk from our Roy Rogers milk glasses.
I'm hoping to make sheriff this time!

ade like the other kids got. We had our own cows, so the milk was raw, not pasturized. It would sit in the thermos all morning and by lunch time, we'd pour it out and a big lump of cream would fall out.

When we got older and didn't want to carry lunch boxes anymore, we got to use sacks or bread wrappers. I'd hide my lunch in my jacket, and some days I'd just dump it in the trash when I got to school. Other times I'd just half-open my lunch and pull out what I was going to have, real quick. Sandy never cared, though. He never threw *his* lunch away, and all through those growing-up years, he just kept on eating and grinning!

Mom and Dad belonged to the Hollywood Christian Group, which started at the Hollywood Presbyterian Church under the direction of Dr. Henrietta Mears. The group provided prayer support and Christian counseling for its members, and they sponsored retreats at Forest Home Christian Conference Center in the mountains near San Bernardino. Every Monday night the group met at a different home for fellowship and to hear a guest speaker.

One warm Monday evening in the autumn of 1953 they held their regular meeting near the pool in our backyard. A special guest was there to lead the meeting, and when it was over, the tall, distinguished-looking young man told my parents he had been invited to conduct a Crusade for Christ in London in the spring.

"Is there anything we can do to help you, Billy?" Dad asked. "We have a pretty good-sized fan club in the British

Isles—our London chapter has about 50,000 fans."

Before the night was over Mom and Dad and their manager, Art Rush, were planning their first overseas tour. They would take their show to the United Kingdom. Beginning in Glasgow, they would appear in many major cities, including Edinburgh, Birmingham, Liverpool, Belfast and Dublin. They would finish their tour by playing in Dublin, Ireland, and then join Billy Graham's crusade in London.

In England Mom and Dad experienced one of the few times they were afraid of the crowds. When they got off the plane, the crowd engulfed them like a wave. By the time they reached their hotel, their hands and arms were bruised, sore and swollen from shaking hands.

They spent six cold and rainy weeks in the United Kingdom, touring damp theatres and dingy castles, and standing in the February rain to greet people. Finally in Liverpool they both ended up in bed with pneumonia.

When word got out that Mom and Dad might not be able to make it to one of their appearances, people began to gather outside the hotel. Some estimates put the crowd at nearly 20,000 people! My folks *did* make their appearance, on stage, though, because in spite of their illness, they were threatened with a lawsuit if they didn't! It was not the first time such a threat had been made, nor would it be the last, but those kinds of experiences represent a side of show business that is painfully real.

But for Mom and Dad, that tour came to represent something quite different, something apart from show business and fans and crowds and unthinking demands. In Scotland my folks did what they tried to do everywhere they went: they visited children in hospitals and in orphanages.

In Edinburgh the chief constable asked them to visit an

orphanage called Dunforth. There they met a young 13-year-old named Marion Fleming. Marion sang for them, and Mom invited her and the matron to join them for lunch the next day. In the hours that followed, Mom and Dad investigated the possibility of adopting Marion, but they discovered they would be required to live in England for two years before they would be eligible.

The way English law works, it is almost impossible for Americans to adopt English children, especially if their parents are still living. Marion's parents were divorced, and both were alive, so the best my folks could do was arrange for a visitor's visa for the summer.

While Mom and Dad were gone, Cheryl and Linda were away at school, so Sandy and I kept ourselves entertained. Dodie was too little to roughhouse with us and to get into mischief, but Sandy and I made up for whatever Dodie couldn't—and probably wouldn't—do.

Whenever my folks were away, they gave Virginia and everyone else who worked for them complete authority over us. There was never a question of whether to discuss a problem with my parents first. My folks believed that transgressions should be handled swiftly, and they didn't want us to think of their homecomings in terms of punishment.

Neither did they want us to think we could raise the roof without having to face the consequences. I think their perspective gave all of us a great sense of continuity and security, because life was much the same whether they were home or not. We had our daily devotions every day, we talked with Virginia at mealtimes, and she disciplined us with consistency and love.

Virginia always made me relish the fact that I was going to get it, and every time, it was the same.

"All right, Dusty, you know what you've done, and you

know what the penalty is. Now I want you to go outside and get me a switch."

I'd go outside and find the feeblest little branch I could find off the peach tree and take it in.

"No sir, that one won't hurt enough to make you remember. You go out there and get me a switch that's worth the getting."

Back out I'd go. I'd have to get the branch ready by stripping all the leaves off of it—then she'd switch me across the back of my thighs. It didn't happen often, but when it did, it was something I remembered.

One day Sandy and I both got it. We had one of those big toy cars with pedals inside. We'd get inside, push the pedals, and the car would go. Sandy and I took it out back, behind some bushes.

Our Swedish gardener, Gus, was very fussy about the yard, especially the roses and the irises, so I'm not sure where we found the old leaves and the dead grass, but we got it all together and put it inside the car and set it on fire.

"Put some more leaves on there, Sandy," I said.

"Okay. Wish we had some frog legs we could cook!"

"Yeah, that would be—oops, Sandy, look out!"

It didn't seem like a big deal to us, but all of a sudden the grass around the car began to smoulder and before we knew it, flames shot up.

"Dusty, look! It's spreading up to them big eucalyptus trees! What are we gonna do?" Sandy moaned.

Sandy and I stood there hopping from one foot to the other for a minute, and then I saw the irises. "Look, Sandy! Get some of these flower leaves. We can beat the fire out with them!" The iris blades were about as effective as the bread I'd tried on the fire in Hollywood Hills. "We gotta get some water," I sputtered.

By that time the smoke was rising and Gus came running up, hollering loud enough to raise the dead. He grabbed a hose and put the fire out, yelling in Swedish all the while, and then he chased us all the way up to the house. Virginia really let us have it that time!

A few days later we went over to Rex Allen's place, which was just down the road from us. Sandy and I loved to go over there because we'd get into terrific dirt clod fights with Rex Jr. and his younger brother, Curtis. One day we were particularly enthusiastic. It was the Rogerses against the Allens, and we were really hurling them back and forth. Rex threw one and hit Sandy in the shoulder. Sandy had a jacket on, but the clod was a big one. Sandy began howling and rubbing his shoulder. I could tell it hurt, and that really made my blood boil.

No more fun and games, now, I decided. I picked up a big clod and let it sail. I clipped Rex Jr. just above the eye. That ended everything. Rex went crying into the house, and a few minutes later his dad came ripping out the door.

"What's the matter with you boys?" he shouted. "Don't you know you could put somebody's eye out like that? You know better than to be throwing rocks. If your daddy were home, he'd tan your hides! I'm going to let Virginia know what's been going on here. Now get this mess cleaned up, and then git!"

The four of us spent about an hour cleaning up the place, and then Sandy and I skedaddled, all right. Rex Sr. was right—Dad would have had our hides, if he'd been home. Because so many of the children he visited in hospitals were accident victims, he and Mom were always talking about safety. They even started a program to give safety awards to schools all over the nation, as a way of encouraging children to think "Safety first."

Sandy and I sweated it out all that afternoon, thinking Rex Allen would call Virginia and tell her about the fight,

71

but this time, we were saved by his mercy—or his faulty memory!

For the next couple of days Sandy and I were on our best behavior. The kind of mischief we did get into never amounted to anything worth fussing over. We'd drag snails out of the iris garden and pour salt on them to see them bubble, or we'd catch flies and eat them. Mom never knew about that, or she'd have nailed us both! One day we found a nest of rats in the barn. They were underneath a bale of hay, and they were still pink—no fur on them. Sandy and I took turns feeding them to the cat.

Every couple of days the phone would ring, and it would be Mom and Dad. If it had been a good day or two, with no spankings, I'd talk to them. If not, I wouldn't.

Finally it was time for Mom and Dad to come home, and not long after that, Marion arrived. It meant another trip to the airport, all clean and gussied up because Virginia insisted. But this time, I didn't mind so much. I was curious about the girl who was going to visit us for the summer.

Marion loved oranges, and Mom gave her a whole bag of them when we met her at the plane. I like to take my time with people, but Sandy ran right up and gave her his hand. She was friendly, and I liked the way she talked. She had a strong Scottish brogue, and it was fun to hear the way she pronounced our names.

"Did you have a nice time on the airplane, Honey?" Mom asked.

"Oh, yes, Mum," Marion answered. "There was a cowboy on the airplane. He sat next to me, and he said the most curious thing!"

"What was that?"

"He asked me, 'Well, little lady, are you traveling all by yourself?' And I said, 'Yes,' and he said, 'Well bless your

Marian showing Mom and Dad how to do the "Highland Shuffle."

Reading the family Bible around the table. (From right) Sandy, Debbie, Dad, Mom, Dodie and me.

little pointed head!'" Marion rubbed the top of her head in bewilderment.

The first few nights she showed us some traditional Scottish dances, including the sword dance and the Highland fling. I stood off and watched from the corner, but Cheryl got to be pretty good at it, and so did Linda.

Marion fit in with us right away, especially at night around the supper table. Perhaps because she had come from an orphanage, she didn't seem to mind the bedlam that supper time could be. She enjoyed the chatter and the silliness.

Like Sandy, Marion had known what it was like to be deprived of food. Although World War II had been over for some time, it had only been a short time since Scotland had stopped rationing food and requiring food coupons. Marion could remember the harshness of the war years, and she was astonished at the amount and the variety of food on our table.

In the early weeks of her visit, in the summer of 1954, Marion couldn't bring herself to eat very much, and yet the two things she couldn't seem to get enough of were oranges and potatoes. After awhile, she realized that she had fierce competition for the potatoes. She had to contend with Sandy and me.

Before we could eat, we prayed together. After folding our hands and bowing our heads, we would take turns thanking God for our various blessings and for the food. In the mornings we shared Scripture verses from a little devotional aid Mom had bought. It was a little plastic loaf of bread containing Scripture verses printed on brightly-colored strips of paper. We took turns reading them as we sat together around our huge round dining room table.

The center of the table was dominated by the biggest lazy Susan I've even seen. George Montgomery made it especially for us. Mom put all the food on the Susan, and we turned it if we wanted anything.

One night Sandy figured out how to have the home court advantage in terms of the mashed potatoes. That night he prayed with his eyes open. With his hands still clasped, he extended his index fingers until they met, and with ever-so-little effort, he used them to turn the Susan slowly until the potatoes were right in front of him.

I couldn't figure out why the potatoes weren't in front of *me* until several days later, when I opened my eyes while we were praying. I joined Sandy's little game, and then Marion figured it out, too. Before we knew it, that Susan was spinning back and forth like the agitator on a washing machine! The next night, Mommy made an announcement.

"Children, I think it's time we started a new family tradition. From now on, we're going to hold hands around the table when we pray, and no one is to let go until Daddy says 'Amen!'"

Summer stretched into winter, and my folks were able to have Marion's visa extended month after month. Finally Marion became their official ward, and she never did go back to Scotland. We began to call her Mimi, and soon she was calling our folks Mommy and Daddy.

Mimi and I got to be good friends. I was eight and she was 13, but we were almost the same size. Out in the yard, we built leaf houses on the ground. We decided where we wanted each room to be, then raked the leaves into the proper floor plans. We did that for hours while Sandy played with his army men.

Even though we liked each other, or perhaps *because* we did, Mimi and I teased each other constantly. I'd wait outside the bathroom door and run by her as she came out after her bath or shower. I'd grab her towel and just keep

75

running. She screamed and hollered every time, but it wasn't long before Mimi realized there's no place for modesty in a family with half-a-dozen kids swarming around all the time.

At dinner Mimi always sat to my left, and she loved carrot strips. She always got the last one, and she waved it in front of my nose to remind me that she was faster on the grab than I was. I tried to get as big a bite of carrot as I could, and one night I bit her fingernail off. A bit closer, and I'd have got her finger, too!

A few nights later we were all especially rowdy, and after a while Mom had had it. "Okay, Dusty, knock it off. Sandy, you, too. Eat your dinner and be quiet."

Sandy went on laughing and grinning, and he shot a pea off his plate at Linda.

"Stop it, Sandy!" Linda insisted. "Mommy, make him stop!"

"Sandy, I told you to knock if off. I'm getting tired of warning you!"

Sandy grinned again, and took another mouthful of potatoes.

"Ouch!" Dodie cried. "Sandy just kicked me!"

"Sandy, this is your last warning," Mom said. "If you don't knock it off, I'm going to drown you in this pitcher of milk."

The tone of Mom's voice meant business, but Sandy wasn't ready to give up. "Aw, Mom, you would never do that!" Laughing, he leaned over and made a face at me. "Nyah, nyah, nyah!" he teased.

Before the rest of us knew what was happening, Mom was out of her seat and around the table, pouring a whole pitcher of milk all over Sandy's head. Pretty soon he was wailing, but she kept pouring.

"Young man," she said, "when I make a promise, I

keep it. Now go get cleaned up; you've had enough dinner for one night!"

Sandy opened his mouth and screamed at her. She screamed back, louder. Sandy took a deep breath and gave it all he had—a long, piercing bellow. Mom half-smiled, took a deep breath, and just about broke all of our eardrums. Sandy stared at her for a minute, shrugged, and left the table.

Sandy and I did our best to have a good time, but we must have driven Mom to distraction. She even kept a long switch in the car so she could reach us while she was driving, and she made good use of it. She'd grab that thing, and one of us would yell, "Hit the deck!" We'd all duck down low, hoping she'd miss us. She rarely missed.

One day I decided I'd had enough. "You don't love me," I declared, "and I'm tired of living here. I'm going to run away!"

"Fine. I'll help you pack."

That wasn't quite the answer I expected from my mom, and I was surprised when she came into my room to help me decide what to take.

I got all packed and then I hung around awhile, but nobody said anything to me. Not one person told me I ought to stay! I decided to talk it over with Mimi.

"Nobody likes me anymore, Mimi."

"I like you, Dusty, but you've been naughty today."

That made me mad, so I pulled out all the punches. "Yeah, well, you're just being mean because you're too short!"

Nothing got to Mimi like that reminder. Although she was 13, she was tiny, and people always thought she was about eight. Tears welled up in her eyes, and I felt terrible because I'd made her cry, but I didn't let her know that.

"Dusty," she said, "you're a naughty little boy!" Then

she turned around and stomped out of the room.

"Yeah, well, I'll show you, Mimi. I'm gonna go outside and eat grass!" I yelled after her. My threat had no effect.

I wandered up to my bedroom so I could talk it over with my brother. "Sandy, nobody likes me anymore."

Sandy grinned, "I do."

"You do? Well, don't you get tired of always getting hit with a switch every time we go in the car?"

"Yeah."

"And aren't you tired of always having nothing but *girls* around?"

"Yeah!"

"And don't you wish we never had to go to school anymore?"

"Yeah!"

"You wanna run away with me, Sandy? We could camp out and go swimming and catch fish."

"Yeah, Dusty! Let's go!"

I don't suppose Sandy really wanted to run away, but he packed a little bag of stuff—mostly army men—and we headed out. We piled our bags into our wagon and started up the hill from our house. When we got to the top of the hill, it seemed like we'd been gone for hours.

"I'm hungry!"

"You're always hungry, Sandy. Did you bring any food?"

"No, didn't you?"

When I said no, I thought Sandy was going to shrivel up and die right there. Pretty soon we were both standing there, bawling, because we were away from home and we had no food. Just then Virginia's old green Chevy pulled up beside us.

"You boys are in a heap of trouble!" she called out the window.

"How come?" I asked.

"Your Daddy's gone and called the sheriff on you. Get in this car, quick-like!"

We scrambled in the back seat and Virginia covered us up with an old blanket. "You boys hush your crying, now," she said. "I'll do my best to sneak you back into the house, but then you're on your own."

Slowly she drove back down the hill to our place. "Okay, the coast is clear. Come on!"

We tiptoed into the house and tore lickety-split down the hall to our rooms.

"Quick! Get under your beds!" Virginia hissed.

By this time, Sandy and I had our own rooms with a little grate between them. We could loosen the screws and crawl from room to room. We decided to get under my bed, and we had just barely made it when I heard my dad cough. He has a distinctive cough, and even today it lets me know when he is in the room.

Soon we saw two pairs of boots, and I heard a voice I'd never heard before.

"All right, Roy," the guy with the black boots was saying, "just where are them two outlaws of yours?"

"Gosh, Sheriff, you know I'd help you if I could. I just don't know where they are!"

"Well, I tell you, Roy, if I ever catch them two boys runnin' away from home, they're goin' to jail and they won't get nothin' to eat but bread and water for the rest of their natural days!"

Sandy and I really ate that up. We knew we'd had it this time. We lay there as still as we could for what seemed like hours—and we never ran away from home again.

Getting ready for action! Dad and Trigger on location.

six

I have the feeling my parents found both humor and truth in Psalm 127:3,5: "Children *are* an heritage of the LORD . . . Happy is the man that hath his quiver full of them."

Dad's quiver was more than full. It was overflowing—not only with children, but also with dogs and pigeons and chickens. It was time to move again, and this time Dad wanted to have livestock—cows and pigs. He wanted a place that was big enough to be self-sustaining, and he was delighted when he found a 138-acre ranch in Chatsworth, California.

It was quite a place. There was a large lake and several ponds, as well as a swimming pool. The Canoga Park High School football team used to have drag races out near the lake. There were separate quarters for the housekeeper and her husband and for the cook, and there was a ranch hands' house. We had a barn, corrals for the horses, pigeon coops, and special shelters for the hunting dogs.

The wood-frame house was accented with lots of brick work, and it was secluded by bushes and trees and other shrubs. Mom and Dad decided to put additions on each end of the house, so it became a sprawling home. You needed roller skates and a map in that place, just to get around. Mom and Dad had the idea of putting in an intercom system, which was really important. Without it, I don't know how we would have managed.

We each had our own bedroom, and the living room had a huge walk-in fireplace made out of petrified wood. We also had a large den, where Dad hung his hunting trophies from Africa. Mom put our family altar in the living room by the front door.

The Western-style kitchen was built to accommodate a large family. We had a walk-in freezer, a large walk-in refrigerator with shelves for storing milk cans and whatnot, another refrigerator for other food items, and a meat closet.

The dining room easily handled our big round table with its lazy Susan, and we had a large aquarium in there, too. The whole house was carpeted in industrial carpet like you find in hotels because with so many children, we needed something that would stand up to the wear and tear.

Way down at the end of the hall was Mom and Dad's room. They had a master suite with sliding glass closet doors, wood paneling, cathedral ceilings, and ivy wall paper. About four steps down and to the left of the master suite was a little television room, and just beyond that was Dad's office. He had a full-time secretary who managed the household needs.

By this time we needed lots of hired help. Betty was a

black woman who did the housework, and Leola was another black woman who did all the cooking. Neither of them wanted the other messing around her territory. If Betty went into the kitchen and lifted the lid on a pan, Leola would grab a fly swatter and chase her through the house. Theirs was a good-natured kind of fussing at each other, though, and both of them were wonderful with us and with their work.

Sandy and I liked Leola. She always smelled of glycerin and rose water, and sometimes she would come out onto the porch and sit and talk with us. She was a great big woman who reminded me a lot of Hattie McDaniel. When she hugged me, she'd darn near push the air right out of me!

Leola loved all of us kids, and every once in a while she'd slip us a piece of candy or gum and say, "Now don't you tell your mama." We'd sneak out back and have it.

One day I went out to play in the backyard, and Leola had about 20 large pans all over the steps. Some of them had flour and some had cornmeal in them. There were black things all over the top of the flour and cornmeal. Leola was out back, shaking some rugs.

"Hey, Leola," I said. "What are you doing?"

"Hey, there, Dusty. Well, there's some boll weevils in the flour and the oatmeal."

"Bugs? Why don't you throw it out?"

"Naw. They don't hurt the flour none. They don't like the sun, so I just set 'em out, and they git up and leave."

Even though Leola liked us, we weren't any more welcome in the kitchen than Betty was. In fact, my sisters never learned to cook until after they were married, because Leola guarded her territory so fiercely. We'd slip our heads just inside the door to see if she were there. She wore slippers but she never quite got them on all the way, and we could hear her padding around. She could never sneak up on us because those slippers gave her away every time.

If Leola were in the kitchen and we told her we wanted a snack, she'd go out to the garden and pick some fresh vegetables. We'd have little strips of carrots and squash sprinkled with salt. When we couldn't hear the slippers, we knew we were safe, so we'd sneak into the kitchen, grab a cookie, and run like the dickens.

She'd come waddling after us with that fly swatter, shouting, "Boy, when I get you, I'm gonna throw your buttocks up to the sun!" She never did catch us, though.

Although Leola was fussy about her kitchen, Mom did the cooking on Leola's days off. Mom wasn't the best cook in the world, probably because she didn't have much time to practice. But one meal she fixed was always my favorite: southern fried chicken. She made corn bread in an iron skillet, and she fixed black-eyed peas and mustard greens. She could fix her "old south recipes" any time she wanted, as far as I was concerned.

Sandy, of course, didn't really have any preferences. Every morning he'd ask the same question: "What's for supper?" No matter what she answered, his response was always the same: "Good!" Only one answer could spoil his whole day.

"Liver."

None of us liked liver. Even Mom disliked it, but because she had once been anemic, she had to eat it. No matter how Leola would try to disguise it, we still hated it. One time Mom decided to try her hand at cooking it, and she figured she'd fix it just like a pot roast. Maybe if she simmered it for a few hours with some tomatoes, it would be good.

Sandy took one bit of it, and for the first time I could

remember, he turned green. He just couldn't understand why Mom would do that to us.

Breakfast always began with oatmeal. When Mom and Dad were first married, one of their sponsors was Quaker Oats. Twice a month they would receive a case of oatmeal. There was no way we could eat all of it, but every morning we had oatmeal before we had anything else.

Sometimes, if it was Leola's day off or if she were on vacation, Virginia would make the oatmeal. It was always a disaster. One day I let it sit there until it was stone cold.

"Come on, Dusty," Mom coaxed. "Two bites."

"Okay," I sighed. I stuck my spoon in and lifted it up. The whole bowlful came up, and the milk ran down into the sides. It wasn't fit for human consumption!

But the oatmeal wasn't the half of it. We also had Puffed Wheat and Puffed Rice—and whatever else Quaker made. When the Nestle company picked up part of the sponsorship, we got cases and cases of Nestle's Quick—chocolate, strawberry, and for a while, even banana flavored. Some of those products started coming when Cheryl was little, and we were still trying to use them up when she got married!

Mom was determined that we would be healthy, so every day we had to have our doses of cod liver oil and Uncle John's Elixer. She'd also make us something she called a "Morning Smile." She mixed orange juice and raw eggs with a tablespoon of honey and some wheat germ, poured it into the blender and whirred it up until it was light and fluffy. I loved that—until she got the idea of hiding our cod liver oil in it. From that time on, it was not a "morning smile" to me—it was a dreadful drink.

Sandy and I both loved the ranch. We had venison to eat from Dad's hunting trips. We crocked our own eggs, putting them in a saline solution so they wouldn't spoil. We butchered our own meat, and we ate our own chickens. My only regret was, with so many children to feed and so much abundance on the ranch, Mom rarely bought us tuna for lunch!

Sandy and I even enjoyed our chores. In addition to the standard chores like keeping our rooms tidy, emptying the trash and carrying our own dirty dishes to the kitchen, we had to haul in the milk from the walk-in cooler every morning. We'd skim the cream off and put it in two separate containers. One container was used for making butter, and one was for coffee, strawberries or cereal. Too little to carry the five-gallon milk cans alone, Sandy would get on one side and I'd get on the other, and we'd carry a can in together and put it in the refrigerator.

One morning we dropped the can. Five gallons of milk went all over the kitchen linoleum, all over the throw rugs, under the refrigerator, under the freezer, under the cupboards, and into the crawl space beneath the kitchenette. Sandy and I tried our best to wipe it up, but five gallons of milk is a *lot* of liquid, and there were places we just couldn't reach. Betty and Leola spent most of the day trying to clean it up, but the kitchen smelled sour for the next couple of weeks.

No matter what the chore, if it was dirty, Sandy and I loved it. One time Dad told us to go out and clean up the pigeon coop. I don't know how clean we got it, but we had great fun slipping around in the droppings! Mom used to get squawking mad at us because when we came in, we reeked!

We also had some wild ducks on the ranch, and they laid their eggs out near the lake or in the pastures. Some of them would be hidden out there for months, and so we never gathered them for eating. On Saturdays Sandy and I would head out to the pasture and get into rotten egg fights. One day we had the time of our lives.

Sandy spotted the first egg when he was about 20 feet away from me. When Sandy took aim, I took a dive—and landed right in a fresh pile of cow pucky. I skidded on my belly through the stuff, and when I stood up, it was ground into my shirt and all the way down my pants.

Looking around, I spied a cow chip. It had a nice crust on the outside, but it was soft enough to be good and mushy in the inside. I took aim at Sandy and let that thing fly. Just as it got close to Sandy, it came apart in the air, and it splattered all over him. We kept that up for hours!

It had rained recently, and there were mud puddles all over the pasture. Sandy and I dove into manure piles and mud puddles until we were unrecognizable. Suddenly Sandy took a dive and disappeared. Pretty soon he was sputtering and calling for help.

I ran over to him, and he was shoulder-deep in a huge mudhole. "Get me outta here, Dusty, or I'm a goner for sure!" he hollered.

No matter how hard he tried, he was stuck. I ran for the barn and hurried back with a rope. Sandy tied it around his chest under his arms, and I pulled and pulled until he was finally able to walk himself out.

We collapsed on the grass next to the hole until we got our breath.

"Know what, Dusty?" Sandy puffed.

"What?"

"I'm starving!"

I could always out-run Sandy, and I took off. Before we got to the house Virginia spotted us, and she made such a racket it wasn't long before Mom came running. She lit into Sandy and me like a hawk after a field mouse. She made us hose off outside, and then she poured disinfectant all over us. We had to take a bath before she'd let us eat anything. We didn't learn from that, though. We had lots of similar fights whenever we could.

At butchering time Dad started with the chickens. He cut their heads off and they ran around, chasing us. When they stopped flopping, Sandy and I helped clean them. We dipped them in hot wax and then, when it had set, we pulled the wax off to get all the feathers out.

One time Dad decided we were big enough to help with the hogs. "Okay, boys," he instructed, "just go into the pigpen and grab those pigs, drag 'em out here, and James will take care of them." James was our Filipino househelper, who was married to our housekeeper, Betty.

It looked easy enough, so Sandy and I jumped in the pigpen. Those pigs dragged us from one end of the pen to the other, squealing the whole time. We never did get hold of them, but we had a great time. We thought it was especially fun, because when we got out, we were covered from top to bottom with muck.

One Monday morning I was out in the front of the house waiting for Virginia. She didn't stay with us on the weekends, so I always waited for her on Mondays. Pretty soon I saw her old green Chevy coming up the driveway. Linda came out onto the porch with me as Virginia walked up to us.

"Dusty and Linda, I have something to tell you." She got down on her knees next to us. Suddenly I felt worried. Virginia looked sad, almost like the day Robin died. She put one arm around each of us and said, "I feel I've done all I can do here. You're all grown up now. You're a young man, now, Dusty—almost nine years old! Linda, you're a young lady. I need to go and help some other little ones."

"What do you mean, Virginia?" I asked.

"I have to go to work for somebody else now. You know that Mr. and Mrs. Allen have a new little baby girl.

88

Her name is Bonita. Now that they've moved to their ranch in Malibu, they need me there."

I was devastated. No other explanation was ever given to me about why Virginia was leaving, and I couldn't understand why Rex Allen's children needed her more than I did. It threw my whole system out of whack. Virginia had been the most consistent guiding influence on my life until that point. She had been a part of my life every day that I could remember, and as much as I loved my mom, Virginia was really the first woman who had mothered me.

I ran to my room and grabbed Peter Cottontail. He was the first toy Dad had ever given me. He had a wind-up music box inside him that played "Peter Cottontail," and I slept with him. When I first got him he wore a pair of white knickers with suspenders. When they wore out Mom made him a little tuxedo with a black bow tie.

I stood him up on the bed and I punched him. He rolled off the bed and onto the floor, and I threw myself on him, punching him until his head came off. I always took all my anguish and frustrations out on Peter Cottontail, and Mom fixed him again and again during those years. I still have him.

After Virginia left I moped around for weeks, and when I got old enough to get around on my own, I often went to the Allens to visit with her. She sized up every girl I dated, and when I married, she gave my bride her seal of approval. Virginia worked for the Allens for the next 15 or 20 years, and not too long after she retired, she died of a massive heart attack.

When Virginia left, Mom and Dad hired another woman to help care for us children. Her name was Pearl White. She had grown up in the Midwest, and she liked kids, but she was strict. She wore a thimble on her middle finger all the time, and when we got out of line, she'd come out of nowhere and ding us in the back of the head with that thimble.

We always watched out for Pearl because she was as silent as a cat, and we could never hear her coming. She moved so fast we hardly knew what hit us. At the table we'd be goofing off. One minute she'd be sitting there and the next minute she'd have flown around that table. *Thunk!* She'd let us have it.

Like Virginia, Pearl didn't stay with us on the weekends, but Betty and James and Leola lived with us all the time. One weekend Mom and Dad were away, and Sandy and I got scared during the night. We'd all gone to bed, and suddenly Sandy started hollering.

"Dusty, Dusty! There's somebody in the closet!" Although Sandy was often frightened by shadows, this time I thought I saw somebody, too. Sandy and I tore out of the room and down the hall, screaming for James. We ran into his room, and he leaped out of bed. Just then James thought he saw something by the screen outside of his window.

James grabbed his gun and ran out of the house in his underwear, shooting and screaming something in Filipino. I can still see him running toward the lake, hollering and firing his gun. He never found anyone. When he got back, Sandy and I were shaking like crazy. The whole thing had scared the dewdrops out of us, and when we refused to go back to our own room, James let us sleep on the floor in his.

Another night not long after that we had a mare in foal. Again we were all in bed, and about one o'clock in the morning we were about knocked out of our beds by a horrible noise. It sounded like a horse screaming. There had been reports of a mountain lion in the area, and we couldn't tell if we were hearing a horse in trouble or a mountain lion screeching.

This time Dad was away, but Mom was home with us.

"Cheryl, get a flashlight," she ordered.

We were all standing around in our pajamas, and Cheryl ran to get her flashlight while Mom grabbed her stage pistol. I don't even know if it was loaded with live ammunition, because she usually kept it full of blanks. Anyway, she and Cheryl set out, tromping across the pasture in search of whatever was making that noise. They were gone about 45 minutes, and when they returned, they hadn't found anything.

I don't know what they would have done if they *had* found a mountain lion. Although Dad is a terrific marksman, Mom never could hit the side of a barn. She just always *looked* real determined!

As the months went by, Pearl began to have health problems. When she had to quit, Mom hired another lady, Ruth Minor. We all called her Granny. She was just one of the boys. She went everywhere we went and joined in all of our games. She drove us to school and was available whenever we needed anything.

I don't remember Granny Minor ever getting mad, and I always had the feeling that she—like all of the people who worked for my parents—would have worked for nothing. They loved us and respected my parents, and it never seemed to me that they considered working for us as "just another job."

And the job was about to become more complicated. Mom and Dad had always been strong supporters of World Vision, and Dr. Bob Pierce, the founder, was a personal friend of theirs. One day he shared with them the plight of thousands of little Korean children, many of whom were unacceptable in their native country because they were of mixed parentage. Their fathers had been United Nations servicemen.

When Mom and Dad saw the pictures of one little girl in particular, we all knew it was only a matter of time before there would be another baby in the house. Dad was about to add another arrow to his quiver.

seven

Sandy and I were in school the day In Ai Lee came to live with us. She arrived on Cheryl's sixteenth birthday, and Mom and Dad took all the girls with them to the airport to get her.

"We're going to call her Deborah Lee," Mom had explained to us that morning. "Debbie for short. She's about three years old, and she only knows a few words in English, like 'Mommy' and 'Daddy.' You kids can help us teach her how to speak English."

I didn't say anything. I put my spoon into my oatmeal and stirred it around for awhile. I always had a hard time warming up to strangers, and I didn't like the idea of a new person living in the family—especially one who couldn't speak English!

If anyone realized what I was thinking, no one tried to

change my mind. No one reminded me that I had loved Robin from the beginning, that Dodie and I got along fine, that Sandy was my best buddy, and that Mimi was special to me. No one reminded me that another child never meant less love in our home, but more of it. It probably wouldn't have mattered if they had. It was something I had to work out for myself.

After breakfast I went up to my room and punched Peter Cottontail around for awhile, then tossed him on the floor by my bed and headed out the door.

That afternoon when I got home from school, I looked for Mom to find out about the new intruder. She was in the den with the girls.

"Is that Korean girl here?" I asked.

"Yes, Dusty, *your sister Debbie* is here."

"Poor little thing," Cheryl said. "She can only speak Korean, and the people at World Vision taught her to say 'Mama' and 'Papa' and to sing 'Jesus Loves Me.' That didn't do her much good today."

"Every time she opened her mouth," Linda put in, "someone grabbed her and took her to the potty, whether she needed to go or not!"

"You should have seen her, Dusty," Mimi chimed in. "She went right to Daddy and just hung on to him for dear life. I think she's going to be a real Daddy's girl!"

"Where is Daddy?" I asked.

"He's out with his pigeons. But guess what!" Cheryl added. "She can imitate! Mimi leaned over to her and said, 'Hello, darling,' and she said it right back!" The girls burst into laughter.

"She has a very low voice for such a tiny little thing," Mimi giggled. "All the way home we got her to imitate us, and every time she said, 'Hello, darling' we cracked up!"

"Where is she?" I asked soberly.

94

"Well, she's had a long trip," Mom said. "She was tired and fussy when we came home, so she and Dodie are taking naps."

"Where's she sleeping?"

"Dodie's in her own bed, and Debbie's in yours."

"In *my* bed?" I whined. "Why does she have to sleep in *my* bed?"

"I was showing her the house, and when we got to your room, she just crawled up on your bed and went to sleep."

I walked down the hall toward my room, and Mom called after me. "Dusty, don't you wake her up!"

Hmpf. I don't know why we have to have another baby— another girl—*around here anyway. Why does she have to take over* my *room?*

When I got to my door, I slid it open slowly, so it wouldn't make any noise. Debbie was curled up on my bed, all right. I walked over toward her to get a better look. She was tinier than I expected, but about the same size as Dodie. Her skin was a pretty light brown, and her hair was almost black.

It was a warm June day, and Debbie's dark hair stuck to her face in little wet ringlets. Tiny beads of perspiration dotted her forehead and her upper lip. For a long time I just stood there, watching her sleep. To this day I can see her lying there, so sweet and vulnerable. Finally I decided it was okay for her to be on my bed. I started to leave, then turned back. I picked up Peter Cottontail and set him down next to her.

"I'll let you borrow him for a little while," I whispered. "But not for keeps."

As soon as she woke up, Debbie went looking for Dad. He was in the den, and when she saw him she crawled up in his lap, patted him on the cheek and put her head on his shoulder. She stayed there until supper time. From then on, we all knew that Mimi was right: Debbie was definitely Daddy's girl. She'd climb up on his lap and rub his hair, and she'd hug him. She was affectionate with all of us, but she and Dad had a certain magic together that everyone recognized.

Before the day was over, we discovered that James could speak enough Korean to get us over the hump. He could tell us what Debbie wanted, but Mom didn't want that to go on for very long.

"Debbie has to learn how to speak English," Mom said. "She lives here now, and it's important that she learn our language."

It didn't take long. Debbie was outgoing and friendly and eager, and she and Dodie became friends right away. Like most siblings, Dodie and Debbie had their share of spats, especially since neither of them had had to learn to share very much. Dodie was five months older than Debbie, so they were both finishing the terrible twos about that time.

One day they were hassling back and forth, and Debbie finally got so flustered she picked up a toy and hit Dodie with it. Just then Mom walked in, and Dodie started crying.

"Debbie hit me!" she wailed.

Debbie looked up at Mom and started jabbering away in Korean, but every few words she'd say, "Dodie . . . Dodie . . . Dodie." She knew she was in trouble, and she'd made up her mind to stand up for herself.

After Debbie was with us for a few weeks, she and Mom were out in the carport. Debbie pointed to the car and started talking a mile-a-minute. Mom knelt down next to her, eye-to-eye, and said, "Debbie, I can't understand you."

Debbie put her hands on her hips and pursed her lips. "Hmpfh!" she grunted, then turned on her heels and stomped into the house. She never spoke another word of Korean after that.

A few weeks later I saw my dad angrier than I had ever seen him. He was pacing the floor in the den, and he was breathing in great gasps. Mom was trying to calm him down.

"If I ever get my hands on that guy, I'll break his face!" Dad shouted, then punched the air with his fist.

"Calm down, Papa," Mom said. I could tell Mom was upset, but Dad was beside himself.

"How could he write something like this?" Dad picked up a magazine and shook it in Mom's face. "Doesn't he realize what this could do to our babies? Who does he think he is?"

By this time Dad was shaking with rage. He began to pace again.

"But, Honey," Mom said, "the children will know it's not true. We'll have a talk with them tonight during our devotions. They won't hear it from anybody else."

"If I ever run into that reporter, even if I have to get up out of a wheelchair when I'm 90 years old, I'll . . . Well, when I get through with him, he'll want to walk West until his hat floats! What does a man like that know about walking the floor all night with a crying baby? Has *he* ever tried to understand a little girl who can't even tell you she needs the bathroom? Does he care about the hurts that happened to Sandy for no reason? What does he know about burying your little girl on her birthday?" Dad's voice broke in pain.

His anger had not subsided, but both he and Mom were in tears, and she put her arms around him. "He doesn't know, Honey," Mom said.

97

I don't think that reporter has any idea of the pain he caused my parents or the damage he could have done to their children when he wrote his article. The essence of his piece was that my dad was adopting children for only one reason: publicity. To this day Dad rankles when he's reminded of that reporter, and although he's a Christian and he knows that Christians must forgive, this is one hurt he has found hard to relinquish to God.

That night we gathered together as usual in the living room near our family altar. It wasn't a real altar, like you find in a church. It was an old record cabinet Mom had covered with a piece of colorful tapestry. She had some incense on it, and some water from the Sea of Galilee that she'd brought back from a trip to the Holy Land. A large open family Bible rested in the center.

There were also some flower petals from Jerusalem and two sculptures: a Madonna and a head of Christ that had a halo. Above the altar was a portrait of Robin, and there was a little kneeling bench in front of it. We always said our prayers there at night before we went to bed.

Because Mom and Dad felt that a personal relationship with God should be the central focus of their lives, Mom made sure the family altar was the central focus in our home. It was visible from several rooms in the house.

Usually Mom led the devotions unless she was out of town, and then Dad led them. This particular night, Mom led them, and Dad was there, but he was subdued. Debbie was sitting in his lap, and he was quiet, never saying a word.

"Before we go to bed tonight," Mom began, "Daddy and I want to have a long talk with you about something very important. It's about adoption. You know that Daddy and Mommy love you all very much.

"Cheryl, before your daddy adopted you, he and your

mommy were very lonely. When you came along, you fit right into the empty space in their lives, and they were so happy. I remember working with your daddy on the set after Linda Lou and Dusty were born and your mommy died. He was always showing pictures of you three, and there was never any difference in how he talked about you. He loved all three of you.

"When Daddy asked me to marry him, I knew that it would be hard for you to accept a new mama and a new brother. I know that Tom seems more like your cousin than your brother because he's never lived with us. But because Tom loved and respected Daddy so much, he started calling him 'Dad.' It's almost like Tom adopted your daddy!

"When Robin came along, she adopted all of us, didn't she? It didn't matter to Robin that all of you had different birth mothers—she loved you anyway, and you loved her.

"After Robin died, we were all so lonely that God sent us Sandy and Dodie, and then Mimi and Debbie. We are the most adopted family I know!

"Some people don't understand about adoption. They don't know how happy a home is when there are lots of children there, and they don't know about our blended family and how we live. When people don't understand, sometimes they say mean things. We just have to forgive them when that happens. Do you understand?"

We all nodded. I looked at Dad. His lips were shut tight, and he was staring at the floor.

"Now I want to read to you from the Bible so we can hear what God has to say about adoption," Mom said as she got the Bible from the altar. "I'm going to read to you from the book of John, which is in the New Testament."

She turned the pages carefully until she found her place, and then she began to read.

He [Jesus] was in the world, and though the world was made through him, the world did not recognize him . . . . Yet to all who received him, to those who believed in his name, he gave the right to become children of God—children born not of natural descent, nor of human decision or a husband's will, but born of God (John 1:10-13, *NIV*).

"That means that when we ask Jesus to make our lives belong to Him, God adopts us as His own children!" Mom explained. "In fact, the apostle Paul telis us that very thing in the letter he wrote to the Christians who were living at Ephesus."

Praise be to the God and Father of our Lord Jesus Christ, who has blessed us in the heavenly realms with every spiritual blessing in Christ. For he chose us in him before the creation of the world to be holy and blameless in his sight. In love he predestined us to be *adopted* as his sons through Jesus Christ, in accordance with his pleasure and will (Eph. 1:3-5, *NIV*, emphasis added).

"It's a very special thing to be adopted, isn't it?" Mom asked us. Then we prayed together. Mom thanked God for adopting Daddy and her, and then she thanked Him for each one of us by name. We said our prayers and went to bed, but that night I wondered about the man who had provoked my dad's wrath.

I never forgot the intensity of my dad's anger, but it wasn't until much later that I realized how much his pain had to do with his profound sense of integrity. Because

Dad has always honored his word, he feels deeply wounded when people misjudge him or misinterpret his intentions. At the same time, he's been around long enough to know that few people still hold to that code of life. It upsets him to think that today's children are often confused by antiheroes and by the good guy who turns out to be evil in the end.

Dad is thin-skinned when it comes to children. He is keenly aware of the impact he has had on young people. Consequently he's fussy about where he goes, what he does, and with whom he is seen, and he carefully guards the image he projects. Because he has been so loved and so honored, it hurts all the more when someone takes a cheap shot at him. Although he doesn't like to let it show, he is tender and sentimental. That day I had a momentary glimpse of something I hadn't realized was there and couldn't even name until many years later: vulnerability.

That a father should be a vulnerable human being, open to pain and disappointment, to loneliness and error, is information most small children rarely comprehend, and I really didn't understand it either. But I began to sense, at that point, that Dad could be disappointed. Not long after that, I felt his disappointment in me.

It started out as a typical boyish prank, and I'm not even sure today whose idea it was. Mom and Dad were determined that we would grow up to be down-to-earth, self-disciplined and responsible people. Even though our parents were famous and had money, they wanted us to learn to take responsibility for our own lives.

Mom and Dad didn't want us to grow up expecting everything to go our way and thinking we could have anything we wanted. That's why we were expected to do chores, to clean up our messes, and to keep our rooms tidy. It's also why we were not allowed an unlimited number of toys. Looking back, I can see how wise they were.

People from all over the world used to send us toys, and we always looked forward to the giant boxes that came at Christmas time from Walt Disney. Walt sent us all kinds of toys—Mickey Mouse watches and figurines of all the cartoon characters. Often it was more than my parents bought for us!

Because we had more toys than we could ever use, most of them were boxed up and sent to hospitals and orphanages. But we were certainly not deprived. In fact, Sandy and I sometimes used to sell our things to the kids at school, until Mom and Dad found out and put a stop to it.

Not too far from the ranch there was a little neighborhood drugstore, and Sandy and I went in there one day to buy some bubble gum. There was a tree-like display with all kinds of nickle-and-dime toys like caps and little cap guns and army men. I reached up and took a cap gun, and Sandy picked out a little plastic submarine. We looked around, and seeing no one, we sneaked out the door. Out on the grass, we looked at our take.

"Gosh, Dusty, wasn't that easy?" Sandy asked.

"Yeah. Tell you what, Sandy. I'll hold this stuff here. You go back and get some more."

"Okay!" Sandy took off, and before I knew it, he was back with a fistful of caps. "Your turn."

I was long on bravery when it was Sandy's turn, but I turned to chicken liver when it was mine. "Naw, Sandy, this time we'll *both* go. We can really clean out the place!"

We went back into the store and took a few more toys, then ran out of the store and around the corner. We were sitting there, looking at all of our new stuff, when suddenly a shadow came over us.

"Hey there, boys. What are you doing?"

I looked up to see the druggist hovering over us. I thought I was dead, right there.

"Uh, nothing," I said.

"What do you have there?"

"Just a few things."

"Where did you get them?"

Sandy just looked at the ground, and I stammered around for a bit.

"You guys want to come with me?"

Oh, no! He's going to call the sheriff for sure, I thought. The druggist marched us back into the store and made us pile all the things on the counter.

"You two just stand right there," he said, leafing through his files. He picked up the telephone. In those days there weren't dials on the phone yet, and you had to tell the operator the number you wanted. I thought I'd lose my lunch when he repeated our number.

"Yes, this is the drugstore. May I please speak to Mr. Rogers? Thank you."

He tapped his pencil on the desk, and Sandy and I looked at each other. Sandy's eyes were as big as an owl's. He was shaking.

"Hello, Roy. Listen, I hate to call you on this, but I thought you'd want to know. Dusty and Sandy are down here, and they just put a few things in their pockets without paying for them. Yes. Okay, I'll do that. Bye."

The druggist put the receiver back into the cradle of the telephone, then turned to face us. "Well, boys, your dad said to hold you here for awhile."

The worst part for me was knowing that Dad knew. It seemed like hours before I heard that cough as he strode in. He glared at Sandy and me, then came over and grabbed us both by the backs of our necks and jerked us up.

103

He stood us up in front of the counter and said, "Now, boys, what do you have to say for yourselves?"

Sandy and I both mumbled something about being sorry.

"How much stuff did they steal?" Dad asked.

The druggist dumped out the evidence on the counter. Dad let out a low whistle. "That's a lot of money. You guys aren't going to be able to pay for that stuff, are you?"

Sandy and I shook our heads back and forth as fast as we could. Dad turned us around and let us both have a hard swat across the back end. Then he took off his belt and spanked us all the way out of the store and into the car. He drove us home in silence.

Back at the house, he grabbed us each by one arm and took us to the back porch. We had a redwood picnic table out there, and he put Sandy on his left and me on his right. Then he folded his belt in half and whacked it over the table. It cracked so loud that Sandy and I both jumped.

"Now that I have your attention," Dad said, "I have a few things to say to you. It's really bad to take what isn't yours. Sooner or later, that'll just put you behind bars somewhere. You start with something small like caps, and then you go on to motorcycles or cars, and the next thing you know, you're in jail.

"But that's not going to happen to you boys, because I'm not going to let it happen. I'm going to whip you. I have to. But this is only the beginning. The next time something like this happens, it's going to be twice as bad as this, and the next time it'll really be a beaut.

"I have to do this because you've done something very wrong. You didn't need those toys, and even though you gave them back, you still did the stealing. This is *never* going to happen again. Now which one of you will be first?"

Dead silence.

104

"Well, Dusty, you're bigger than Sandy, and older, so you can be first." He picked me up and bent me over his knee. I decided I wouldn't cry, no matter what.

"Whap!"

Nothing.

"Whap!"

Nothing. Dad decided if I didn't cry, I wouldn't learn anything, and he kept whapping until I finally let out a howl.

Sandy was shaking all over, but he figured out right away the secret to a short spanking. The first swat, he let out a bellow that could be heard from Chatsworth to Azusa. But Dad hit him a few more times, just to make the punishments equal.

Then Dad put his arms around both of us and said, "I sure hated to do that. But I'm your daddy, and it's me who has to show you right from wrong."

I never wanted Dad to be mad at me again—and it wasn't because I was afraid of him. Like any kid, I never wanted to be spanked. But there was something in Dad's voice this time besides anger. It was disappointment.

I knew being Roy Rogers's son meant that others expected me to behave differently. Whatever I did, I didn't want him to be ashamed of me, and I didn't want people to think bad of him because of me. Those thoughts remain very much a part of me today. My parents have spent more than 50 years laying down a standard, a set of values. For me the question is, do I measure up?

In a sense, being the son of Roy Rogers has prepared me for being a Christian. Mom always used to say to me, "Dusty, you have to watch what you do because your life is the only Bible some people are ever going to read."

I realize there's tremendous truth in that. How many times do people say they don't want to become Christians because of what they have observed in the lives of other Christians? How often do people say they would rather do business with a non-Christian than a Christian? That wounds me because I know they are interpreting what God is like on the basis of what they have seen in the lives of some of His unruly children.

Such thinking gives me a double responsibility: living a life that honors both my heavenly Father and my earthly one. I am thankful for parents who cared enough about me to teach me these values and to live lives that taught me, by example, the way of integrity.

eight

Sandy and I both had problems in school. Our grades were awful. Sandy's learning disabilities were more pronounced than mine, and they had even been foretold in the results of the physical examinations he had when he first came to our family. Sandy would be a slow learner, and there would be a limit to what he could learn.

In those days, little sympathy was given to children who, for whatever reasons, were having problems in school. The teachers were sometimes impatient with us, and we were frustrated, too. When we acted out our frustrations, our teachers called our parents.

One day Mom and Dad called Sandy and me into the den for a talk. "Boys, we want to talk with you about something," Mom began. "You know that your papa and I are away a lot these days, especially during the week. And you know that you've both had some problems at school.

Papa and I have talked it over, and we've decided to try you at a new school."

Sandy and I hung our heads and didn't say anything. I hated going to a new school—or even starting school each fall. I dreaded roll call, when the teacher said, "Roy Rogers, Jr."

I answered, "Here" as quickly as I could, and stared at the floor. Everyone turned around and looked for me. "Where is he?" they whispered. Then, out on the playground, they came up to me and said, "Roy Rogers, huh? You don't look like much of a cowboy." A new school would mean going through that all over again.

"We're going to send you to a fine school," Mom was saying. "We've asked a lot of people about it, and we hear that it's a really good school. You'll stay there during the week, and you can come home on the weekends."

"You're going to *leave* us there?" Sandy asked. His chin was trembling.

"Just on weekdays, Honey." Mom put her arm around him. "It's too far to come home every day, and besides, Daddy and I won't be here most of the time during the week, anyway. We'll pick you up on Fridays right after school and take you back on Sunday nights. It's a military school, Sandy. You'll like that, because you like to play army. At the academy, you'll get to advance in rank, and you'll even have a uniform!"

Sandy did perk up at that, because he was interested in the military. Even though he was little, he loved the Civil War and knew a lot about the famous battles. Mom had even found him a little Civil War uniform, which he loved. He called himself the "Little Rebel."

"Are you mad at us because our grades are bad?" I asked.

"No, Honey. But maybe the discipline at military

108

We loved coming home for the weekends from the
academy (fifth grade).

school and being away from home will help you. Maybe being at home with the girls and having Mom and Dad away so much is keeping you from doing your best. Maybe you're just not getting the best education in the school you're going to. We want to see if this will help, but we're not mad at you, Honey."

The following Sunday afternoon Mom took us to the school in Altadena, California. It was a long drive, and we could see Mom's point: it would be too far to come home every day. The school was completely secluded by trees so it couldn't be seen from outside the gate. None of the buildings was visible from the street. The closed-in play areas were surrounded by chain-link fencing covered with thick vines. The place looked like a dungeon.

Mom took us to the administration office, where we were greeted by the headmaster. The Colonel was a retired Marine who had been wounded during World War II. He'd caught a bayonette in the leg, so he had a pronounced limp. He was a huge man, but not solid with muscle. His body jiggled with fat.

"No, Mrs. Rogers, we don't encourage the parents to go to the barracks with the boys. It just makes the parting that much harder. Why don't you just say good-bye here, and then we'll get them settled. I'll have one of the cadets show them around the academy, and we'll start them in class first thing in the morning. Tell your mother good-bye, boys. She'll be here Friday to get you."

Mom kissed us and hugged us, and then she left. Sandy was teary, but then the cadet came to take us to the barracks. We couldn't believe it! The room was stark, with walls like paper. There were holes in some of the walls, and a bug light hung from the ceiling. I missed the warm wood paneling, my soft chenile bedspread, and the curtains in my own room at home.

Sandy and I always got cold at night. The barracks were cold and drafty. One of us got the idea that we could fill the cracks and holes with toothpaste to stop the cold from coming in, but it didn't work.

"Dusty?" Sandy asked one night.

"Yeah, Sandy?"

"You don't think Mom and Dad are gonna dump us here forever, do you?"

"Of course not!" And I didn't think that. But I think it ran through Sandy's mind a lot. Having been abandoned three times before, he never did feel as secure as the rest of us, and I'm not sure he ever resolved those feelings of abandonment.

By Friday we were more than ready to come home. Mom picked us up at the gate, and Sandy and I both started talking at once.

"Mom, it's awful here!" I started.

"Yeah! The Colonel is mean! He takes candy from the kids!"

"Well," Mom answered, "I'm sure he doesn't want you guys eating candy during school. You'll get used to the rules after awhile."

"Huh uh, Mom. He's just mean," I said. "And the other teachers are, too. I think one of them is a Russian spy! He keeps putting his hands in his arm pits and smelling them!"

"You get demerits if your buckle isn't shined or if your zipper is down," Sandy added.

"Yeah, and the teachers have these paddles with holes in them, and they give swats," I put in.

"If kids are naughty, they need to be disciplined, Dusty. You know that you get spankings at home when you disobey," Mom replied. "They're just trying to help you grow up, that's all."

"Nah, Mom, it's not like that," I answered. "They beat you on your hands—on the palms of your hands or across your knuckles."

We complained all the way home, and Mom tried to soothe us. Everyone disciplines differently, she explained, and it always seems bad when someone you don't know is upset with you. We would get used to it.

The weekend was wonderful. Sandy and I roamed all over the ranch, savoring everything. We ran wild outside, and inside we crawled back and forth through the grate between our rooms. Leola even gave us extra cookies once in a while, and at night we fell into our own beds thinking they were the most comfortable beds in the world. Peter Cottontail was waiting there for me, and I alternately beat him up and cuddled him.

We watched television on Friday nights, then got up early on Saturdays to watch cartoons and Mom and Dad's program. We threw ourselves all over the furniture and the floor, copying the stunts. We liked Howdy Doody, and on Saturday nights we loved to watch the wrestling matches.

On Saturday afternoons Dad took us over to his gun range in Chatsworth, and we practiced target shooting. No matter what we did during the day, by Saturday night we were so wild we were almost beyond redemption. We threw ourselves on the floor, rolling and hollering, really tearing up the place.

"Okay, boys. Enough's enough!" Mom shouted one night.

We ignored her.

"Knock it off!"

We kept it up. Mom came close and bellowed in our ears, "I said stop it!" We didn't.

Suddenly we heard an explosion. It was the loudest

bang I'd ever heard! Instantly Sandy and I stopped wrestling and sat up. Sandy was shaking and his eyes were darting back and forth. I must have looked the same. Then we saw her. Mom was standing there like a statue, with her stage pistol pointed to the ceiling. She was staring at us with murder in her eyes. I don't think we would have been surprised at all if smoke had come out of her nose.

"I *said,*" she whispered through clenched teeth, "it's time to stop. Now," and this time she shook the rafters with her voice, "*be quiet!*"

This time we believed her.

Sundays were always special. We all got up early because it took so long to get seven of us ready for Sunday School. Mom fixed breakfast rolls and milk, and then we headed out for church in the station wagon. There was never any question about whether or not to go to church—we all expected to go.

After church we went out for Sunday dinner. It was wild—all nine of us, with high chairs for the little girls. We usually went some place where Sandy and I could have all the fried chicken we could eat, and sometimes we were scattered all over the restaurant. The big girls took charge of the little girls, and Mom and Dad took charge of Sandy and me.

Because Sunday was the only day we were all likely to be home, we couldn't go anywhere. We had to stick around the ranch. But we could have friends over and do whatever we wanted. Mom could kick back and relax, and she would nap or read.

Leola was off on Sundays, too, so we were free to do whatever we wanted in the kitchen. I was about eight when I started making popcorn for everyone. I did it up right—lots of popcorn with butter and garlic salt and parmesan cheese. That became my regular job, and I made popcorn for everyone until I grew up and was out on my own. I'm still the popcorn maker for my own family.

Sunday dinner seemed to wear off for everyone about the same time, and we'd all hit the kitchen at once. Mom and Dad were sponsored by a cereal company then, so there were always boxes of corn flakes and Raisin Bran, and of course, Nestlē Quik.

Sandy would mix a box of Quik with a gallon of milk in a large salad bowl then throw a box of cereal on top. That guy would eat anything—*anything*.

Late one Sunday afternoon our friend Joe Espetalier came by. Joe and Dad were members of the Masonic Temple in Hollywood. Not only did Joe guide Dad through his Masonic activities, but he also invested a lot of time in Sandy and me. Joe was a bachelor, and when Virginia Peck was still with us, I had ideas about getting them together. They were good friends, but nothing ever came of my matchmaking.

Joe showed up every Sunday afternoon and relaxed with the folks, then drove Sandy and me back to the academy because it was near his own home. As soon as it was time to go back, Sandy and I started crying.

"Please don't make us go, Mommy," Sandy begged. "Please let us stay here."

"Now Sandy, it'll be all right," Mom tried to soothe him. "You did a good job on your papers at school this week, and you'll be fine. Dusty's with you."

We climbed into the car and watched out the window as Joe drove out of the driveway. We watched until the ranch was out of our sight, and then we cried all the way to Altadena. Joe tried to cheer us up.

"Now, fellas," he'd say, "everyone gets a little homesick once in awhile. But your folks wouldn't send you any place that wasn't good for you. This school costs a lot of

114

money. It can't be as bad as all that."

But it was. It was like a reformatory. As soon as we got inside the gate and Joe drove away, we were searched. Any candy or other treats were confiscated and given to the Colonel.

Twice a week or so we could send letters home, and Mom wrote or called us a couple of times a week. Sometimes she sent us packages with little treats, and she also sent vitamins with us. She was especially picky about the vitamins because of Sandy's medical history. If we got out of line, our treats were confiscated.

The Colonel's inner office was stacked with candy. I think if *Star Wars* had been around then, we'd all have called the Colonel "Jobba the Hut," because he was so fat and so cruel.

I tried to keep my nose clean and stay out of trouble, but Sandy was always catching it. He'd get swats with the paddles and demerits because he had a serious bed-wetting problem he was never able to outgrow. Mom had taken him to doctor after doctor, and nothing could be done.

For nearly a year we agonized at that place. Week after week we tried to tell Mom and Dad, and every Sunday we poured our hearts out to Joe. Once Mom did call the school. The Colonel invited her out, and he took her on a tour of the officers' quarters and the administration building. Seeing nothing amiss, she was more convinced than ever that Sandy and I were merely homesick.

One of the boys had a problem with seizures. I tried to be nice to him because the other kids didn't understand. I knew from Robin that his disability didn't keep him from being an okay person with lots of special needs, and I was concerned about him. One day he told me something that really upset me.

115

"The doctor gave me some medicine," he told me. "It's supposed to keep me from having seizures."

"Hey, that's great!" I said.

"Yeah, but last week I got some demerits, and the Colonel took my medicine away. He said if I can't behave, I can't have my medicine."

"Did you write your mom and tell her?"

"Yeah. She never answered my letter. Do you think she got it, Dusty?"

I didn't think so. Sandy and I realized what whenever we wrote any kind of complaint in our letters, Mom didn't get them. Our mail was being watched very carefully.

One day not long after that Sandy got himself in trouble. I don't even remember what he did, but whatever it was, the Colonel was angry. He ordered that Sandy would not receive his vitamins until further notice.

That night in the mess hall, we got to talking. "Look at this food," someone said.

Ol' steel-stomach smiled. "Aw, it isn't that bad. It's chicken tetrazzini!"

"Yeah," said one of the guys, "but look! Mine has a worm in it!"

We all looked. It sure did look like a worm. I looked around to see if anyone was watching.

"Here. Give it to me. Tomorrow's Friday. I'll smuggle it home and tell my folks."

I stuffed the worm in my pocket. *Now they'll have to believe me,* I thought. *This time, I have proof.*

I showed the worm to Dad as soon as I got home.

"Oh, Dusty!" he said, shaking his head. "You've lived on this ranch long enough, and you've helped with the chickens long enough to know that this is probably a piece of intestine or a blood vessel of some kind. Your imagination is running away with you, boy!"

I was crushed. Dad didn't believe me. Mom didn't believe me. *When I grow up,* I told myself, *I'm really going to listen to my kids.*

Now that I am an adult with children of my own, I realize how easy it is to dismiss the things that children say. Because children have vivid imaginations and because their logic is sometimes faulty, adults tend to disregard statements that can be strong warnings about something that is truly amiss.

Today, child abuse experts say that it is important to believe the things children say because they rarely make up stories about abuse. In fact, many do *not* tell simply because they do not expect to be believed. Educators who understand this are beginning to teach children to tell, and to keep telling, until somebody finally hears them.

That's what Sandy and I did. And finally, somebody heard. I don't know if it was because Sandy told Joe about the vitamins, or if it was because Mom became concerned about missing so many letters. I don't know what brought about the change, but one day Mom came and picked us up from the academy and said we didn't have to go back. That was the best news I ever received.

A family photo taken in a Columbus, Ohio hotel.
(Clockwise from left) Dad, Cheryl, Linda, Marian,
Mom, Sandy, Dodie, Debbie and me.

nine

Only one word can describe our summers. Chaotic. Summertime is rodeo time, fair time, personal appearance time, and so instead of family vacations or lazy days on the beach, the Rogers family went on the road. All of us were included in the act.

Weeks before it was time to leave, Mom started making lists. There were lists of the things she had to do, like costume fittings for herself and trips to the tailor for each of us for special fittings for our show clothes. The show clothes had to be shipped about two weeks before we were scheduled for an appearance, so Mom always scratched those chores off her list first.

There were lists for what Dad had to do. There were lists of what to take. All seven of us kids had our own separate lists—two each. One was for show clothes, and the other was for regular clothes.

The lists included everything each person needed, including toiletries like toothbrushes and deodorant. The girls' lists even included the number of bobby pins they could take! Mom also listed the number and color of pairs of socks and underwear, and it was our responsibility to count everything before we left each hotel, so we didn't leave anything in the drawers. As we grew older it became our responsibility to pack our own things, and once everything was packed, we were not allowed to touch any of it. Woe betide the person who tried.

When it was time to leave, we all lined up, and Mom counted noses.

"One, two, three, four, five, six, seven. Okay, let's go. Dusty, you take Sandy's hand. Sandy, you take Debbie's. Debbie, you take Dodie's hand. You big girls, you take the little ones."

Then through the airports we would go, along with the other members of the troupe. The wives of some of the men who were part of the show would help ride herd on us, and quiet, shy Mary Jo Rush, the wife of Dad's manager, often ended up with one of the little girls on her lap.

On the airplane it was frantic, and because of the size of our family and the troupe, we about filled it with the Rogers entourage. The stewardesses always did their best to keep things from getting boring. One time a stewardess let Sandy and Debbie deliver the finger sandwiches. I felt slighted, and I stewed about that for 20 minutes. Then Sandy said he was thirsty, and I got a splendid idea.

"I'll go get you a drink, Sandy!" I volunteered. I got up and made my way to the restroom at the back of the airplane. I had a balloon in my pocket, so I squirted some liquid handsoap into it, then hooked it on the water spout and filled it with water. That made bubbles, so I eased them out and wiped the balloon off with paper towels.

I made my way back to Sandy and handed him the concoction. "Here, Sandy. It's got pop in it!"

He took a big swig, and I thought he was going to burst. Soap bubbles foamed around Sandy's mouth, and he started coughing and choking.

"What's the matter, Sandy?" Dad asked. "Are you all right?"

"Dusty put s-s-soap in my water!" he sputtered, and then he began to wail in a low, moaning voice.

Dad shot out of his seat like a rocket and grabbed me by the back of my neck. He steered me all the way down the aisle to the bathroom, where he blistered my bottom. He was so mad he could hardly speak.

"Do you like—you did a—how could you—that could have made Sandy sick! Soap! Dusty!" he sputtered. "You did a bad thing to your brother, and I'm disgusted with you! Let's see how you like soap." He washed my mouth out with soap and then he dragged me, coughing and crying, back to my seat.

By the time we reached the airport Sandy and Dad had both forgiven me, and we were all friends again. We were met by hundreds of fans and a police escort. We liked that! They took us to our hotel, where we had a suite of rooms.

On days when the opening show was in the evening, Mom would try to get us to take a nap. Other days we did two shows—an afternoon matinee and then the evening performance. Sometimes the little girls would sleep in the late afternoon, but Sandy and I wrestled on the beds and watched television with the big girls. Late in the afternoon Mom made us all wash and dress for dinner. Our rooms looked worse than a disaster movie every day when we left them. No matter how hard Mom tried to keep us orderly, it was impossible. There were too many of us.

While Mom and Dad dressed, we went down to the dining room and ordered. Whenever we could get away with it, we ordered the most expensive things on the menu. Dad always turned red when he saw our plates.

"If you guys don't eat every bite of that," he'd say, "I'm going to cloud up and rain all over you!"

"Think of all those children who are starving in Asia and Africa!" Mom scolded. "Don't you let any of this go to waste." Not that that was a problem—Sandy always made sure of that!

When everyone had been served, we said grace and ate dinner. Mom sat between Sandy and me, and Cheryl took charge of Debbie while Mimi took care of Dodie. Dad sat at the other end of the table. Even with that much supervision, the level of noise rose louder and louder, and Mom tried to quiet us.

"If everyone is talking, no one is eating," she said.

When the noise didn't settle, she started singing to shush us. Pretty soon everyone in the dining room was looking at us, and we all fell silent.

"Thank you," Mom said, smiling.

Why do kids do things in public they would never do at home? It's the classic question every parent asks sooner or later, but I think Mom figured it out. She decided it was directly related to her threat, "Just wait 'til we get back to our room!" We acted up in public because we didn't expect her to discipline us in public. We thought wrong.

One night at dinner Sandy and I started teasing each other. Mom was sitting between us as usual, and she told us to knock it off. We kept it up, and the rest of the kids were warning us to stop.

Suddenly I felt Mom grab a small piece of skin on my leg, just above my knee. I tried to keep quiet, and I was making faces, but Sandy started moaning in that low voice of his, and the more Mom pinched, the louder Sandy moaned. Everyone in the room was staring at him, and he continued to howl. From where we were sitting, no one could see what was bothering him, and Mom just sat there smiling sweetly.

By this time I'd begun to whimper, too, and the people kept looking at Sandy and me.

"I told you boys to be quiet," Mom said softly, still wearing her biggest smile, "Now will you be quiet?"

Sandy and I nodded rapidly, the tears rolling down our faces. Sandy kept moaning and kept whimpering. Mom and Dad just smiled and talked to each other in low voices. I'm certain the other dining room customers pitied them for having such an unruly mob of youngsters, but that took care of acting up at the table for the rest of our trip!

After supper we all paraded to the elevator and to our rooms, where we dressed in our show clothes. A flurry of orders always accompanied this ritual.

"Sandy, don't cross your eyes. They'll get stuck that way. Dusty, tuck your shirt in. Be sure to put clean underwear on in case we get in an accident. Line up! Sandy, your boots are on the wrong feet! Dusty, have Mimi help you with your tie. Cheryl, help little Debbie with her boots. Sandy, for heaven's sake, zip your britches!"

At last we were ready. We'd pass inspection, and then it would be time to go. Another police escort took us to the fairgrounds, and we arrived about 45 minutes before show time.

Dad and the Sons of the Pioneers went on first, doing their songs and Dad's target shooting. If it was a place with an arena, Dad did a routine with Trigger or with Trigger, Jr. Then Mom joined him, and they sang together and did their routine.

That's a long time for little kids to wait, so there was

soda pop for us and other snacks, and the little girls would run around backstage, chasing each other. Sandy and I often got into wrestling matches, and by the time it was our turn to go on stage, we were a mess. Hair mussed up. Zippers undone. Shirts hanging out. Neckties untied.

There was always someone to keep an eye on us while Mom and Dad were performing, and they would do a quick fix-up on us just before Mom called us out on stage. We went out one at a time. The big girls sang with Mom and Dad, usually something like "The Bible Tells Me So":

Have faith, hope, and charity
That's the way to live successfully
How do I know? The Bible tells me so!
Be good to your enemies
That's the way to live successfully,
How do I know? The Bible tells me so![1]

Then the little girls went out. Dodie sang a song with Dad. They called it "Chicky-Whikkie Choctaw." Then Debbie sang "Jesus Loves Me" in Korean.

Dad told a story about me, and whether or not it was true didn't seem to matter; the audiences loved it.

"You know, pardners, the Rogers family always goes to church and Sunday School every Sunday morning. The children like Sunday School, but they don't always understand the big messages in the sermons. Last week we went to church, and the minister spoke about the passage in the Bible that says, 'From dust thou art, and to dust thou shalt return.'

"When we got home from church, Dusty and Sandy were playing in their bedroom, and Dusty noticed some dust under his bed. He came tearing down the stairs.

"'Daddy! Daddy!' he shouted at me. 'There's somebody under my bed, and I don't know if he's coming' or goin'!'"

Just then Sandy and I ran out, and the whole family sang, "Oh Be Careful Little Hands, What You Do." Debbie had a deep, low voice, and she never learned to sing the words right. She'd sing, "what it do," and really hit the "do" low. Everyone would laugh. On top of that, poor ol' Sandy never could carry a tune, so it was quite a number.

We finished off with a patriotic medley of some kind, and at the end Dad sometimes picked Sandy up, sometimes me, and we'd all sing "Happy Trails." Mom had written it in 20 minutes one afternoon when they needed a song for a show. No one realized then that it would become my parents' theme song, or how much it would typify our lives:

Some trails are happy ones, others are blue.
It's the way you ride the trail that counts;
Here's a happy one for you.
Happy trails to you until we meet again.
Happy trails to you, keep smilin' until then.
Who cares about the clouds when we're together?
Just sing a song and bring the sunny weather.
Happy trails to you 'till we meet again. [2]

One night, years later, I was doing a show in Ohio, sharing stories about our family, and singing. Dad was watching backstage. When it was time to finish, I told about singing "Happy Trails" in my Dad's arms, and then I started to sing. Suddenly Dad came running out from backstage and jumped into my arms. It brought the house down!

It was always late at night when we finished—the

shows lasted about two hours—and we fell into bed as soon as we got back to the hotel. But Sandy always had a hard time at night. The old night terrors continued to plague him. One night, he woke me up about 1:00 in the morning.

"Dusty! There's someone in the room!"

"Oh, Sandy, you're always saying that!" I groaned. "Go back to sleep!"

"No, Dusty. This is real. Listen!"

I sighed and sat up. Sure enough, I heard a rustling sound. "Quick, Sandy, turn the light on!"

Sandy turned the light on just in time to see a bat fly into the other room! Sandy started screaming and ran out into the hall. I grabbed a coat hanger and chased the bat into the other room. I could hear Sandy running up and down the hall outside, screaming.

Suddenly Dad burst into the room. "What in blazes is going on in here?" he bellowed.

"It's a bat, Dad," I shouted.

Dad grabbed the hanger and took care of the bat with it. Sandy was still tearing up and down the hall, and by this time the entire floor was awake. People were standing in their doorways, and the hotel manager and the bell captain had come up. The manager was apologetic about the bat, but I wonder now if he was beginning to question what he had done to deserve the Rogers family at his hotel!

A few nights later we got back to the hotel really late, and Sandy was done in. We all got our pajamas on and crawled into bed, but somehow in the confusion of so many people, Sandy was overlooked. In the morning when we got up, Sandy was sound asleep in bed, all right, but he was wearing his show clothes. His bed-wetting problem was still with him, and he was soaked.

I thought Mom would have a stroke. She peeled

Sandy's tailor-made costume off of him and started chasing him up and down the hall, snapping him with his pants.

"Mrs. Rogers! What are you doing? Why are you so mad?" a maid asked.

"Oh, I'm just furious at that boy," Mom panted. "He wore his best clothes to bed last night, and now they're ruined! These are the only good pants he has!"

"If he's still wetting the bed when he's 65," said the maid, "then you can be mad at him. The hotel cleaners can repair the damage and have the clothes ready in plenty of time for this evening's show."

The maid, of course, had no idea of the struggle Mom was having with Sandy's bed-wetting problem. At home, she had purchased one of those mats that sounds an alarm and sets a bright light off at the first hint of moisture. The first night it woke Sandy up, all right. After that, he slept right through it, and the rest of the household woke up instead.

Mom had also tried a reward system. If he stayed dry, she gave him a present. It didn't work. She tried shaming him. She tried getting him up every two hours. She prayed. She took him to doctors, specialists, urologists. She tried pills and other medicinal mixtures. She asked everyone she could ask about how to help Sandy.

One day in Chatsworth some carpenters were doing some work on the house, and Mom got to talking with the contractor.

"You ought to do what my mom did," the contractor told her. "It's an old country remedy."

"I'm ready to try *anything*," Mom said.

"Okay! Catch a little field mouse, and skin it. Make a little stew out of it, and feed it to the boy. He'll never wet the bed again! My mother tried it with me, and it broke me of the problem!"

127

Mom was horrified. "You're kidding! I could never do such a thing!"

Betty, the housekeeper, had overheard the conversation. "I could do it, Mrs. Rogers!" she said. "It really is an old country remedy, just like the man said. It works!"

That Mom should give in to such an idea is proof of her desperation. Poor Sandy was so humiliated by his problem, and she was so tired of all the laundry, she simply wanted him free from it forever.

Later that week Betty set a trap and caught a field mouse. She made a succulent stew out of him, and Leola made stew that night for the rest of us. No one cracked a smile, but Sandy raved about the stew—he didn't know his was any different. He wet the bed again that night.

Mom felt awful. After that, she began to accept Sandy's problem with bed-wetting, and she tried not to be impatient with him. Sandy continued to be a bed-wetter, and even after he was in the Army, he got up before reveille every morning and made his bedroll so no one would know. Since then, Mom has come to understand that Sandy's problem was connected with his brain damage. She's worked hard at forgiving herself for the mistakes she believes she made in dealing with this particular handicap.

But in the meantime there were the nights on the road, and the accidents, and like any normal human being, Mom sometimes lost her cool about it. After the incident with the show clothes, she resolved again to accept what she couldn't change and to change what she could. From then on, she made sure we all left our show clothes at the fairgrounds.

In the mornings after the shows, we all ate breakfast in the hotel dining room while the hotel maids tried to make some kind of order out of the chaos in our rooms. After breakfast it was time to connect with our police escort again, and we spent the day visiting newspaper offices, hospitals, orphanages, and attending luncheons, special presentations and other publicity stuff. There were always photo sessions.

Cheryl loved the photo sessions because she was so much into her part: "the daughter of . . . . " Linda often cried because she hated to have her picture taken, and I sometimes made faces. The rest of the kids seemed to take it in stride, even though it sometimes seemed like we spent most of the summer in front of the camera. In the background people said things like, "Oh, aren't they cute!" and "How do you suppose she manages?"

Mom and Dad kept tight security on us. Even though the problem of child stealing did not appear to be as widespread then as it is today, Mom and Dad had never forgotten the tragic kidnapping and murder of the Lindbergh baby. They knew that children of public figures can be especially vulnerable.

If it looked like the crush of people could endanger us, we were kept away from the show. At the rodeos there were plenty of things to see, like riding contests, and there were carnival rides and exhibits, but we were not allowed to wander off by ourselves. We were always supervised by adults. It was fun sometimes, but most fairs and rodeos are alike, and it got old mighty fast.

To be fair to us, Mom insisted that we be paid wherever we performed. She reminded the people in charge that we had to have special clothes and that we had to be made up for two performances each day. She never used our money to cover those costs, though. Instead, she banked it.

Each of us had our own savings account, but we weren't allowed to touch it until we were old enough for our first major purchase. Mom told us we could use it for a car or for furthering our education, and I think we all used our show money for our first cars.

One time we were at a state fair, and Dad was really feeling the need just to relax and enjoy himself. The parade officials helped him into a fireman's uniform, and the make-up people made him up with a mustache and a beard so he could go out unrecognized. It didn't work. Perhaps he said something or started humming, or maybe it was the way he carried himself. Perhaps it was his boots. Whatever it was, people began to recognize him, and he was soon swamped with autograph seekers.

Every summer held a different adventure for us. One year we played the Wisconsin State Fair, and it rained and rained for five straight days. The weatherman said it rained nine inches during those five days, and the streets were flooding.

One afternoon we were on stage singing "California, Here I Come!" There was a big overhead tarp to protect us from the weather, and every three or four minutes the stage hands would push up on the tarp to make the water run down the sides.

Right in the middle of the song we heard a tearing sound. The tarp gave way under the load of water, which poured down on the orchestra behind us. All the sheet music went flying all over the stage.

Most of the time, though, it was monotonous, and one day Dad decided Sandy and I needed a diversion. Mom didn't like the idea, but Dad overruled her and bought us four male white rats. He said it would be good for us to take care of them. We kept them in a little bird cage.

Sandy and I enjoyed them. We'd sneak them into the hotel rooms, and they kept us busy during the long waits between acts. But one day we noticed that two of the rats were getting really fat.

130

"You have to stop feeding them so much, boys," Dad explained. "Are you sure the other two are getting their share?" We were sure.

Finally it was time to go back home. We packed up and headed for the airport. By that time it was obvious that our two overweight rats were females, and Sandy and I didn't want them to go in the luggage hold. We put the females in one shoe box and the males in another, and we poked pinholes in the boxes so they could breathe. We carried them on the plane with us.

Somewhere over the Rockies both of those rats decided to give birth. The babies all started squeaking, and whenever the stewardess came down the aisle for anything, Sandy and I started making squeaking noises so she wouldn't get suspicious. When we got on the plane that day we had four rats. When we got off, we had 32.

We always arrived home from the summer tour after school started. I hated that, because it meant always being the new kid at school, year after year. The September after Mom and Dad pulled us out of the military school was no exception, and this time, it almost seemed worse. Mom and Dad decided to try us out in public school again.

Notes

1. Written by Dale Evans. Used by permission.
2. "Happy Trails," by Dale Evans. Used by permission.

ten

We all had our own problems adjusting to school, especially when the other kids didn't really know us. Their expectations of us, like the public image of our parents, were larger than life. At dinner we sometimes complained about the way the other kids treated us.

"I was going down the stairway," Mimi said one night, "and I heard some kids say something about Roy Rogers' daughter being a creep. I couldn't believe it!" Mimi took an angry bite from her carrot stick.

"I can believe it," Cheryl said. "No matter what people decide about us, I'm never surprised anymore. A couple of weeks ago I overheard a girl say she'd been going to school with me, and that I'm nothing but a stuck-up b____!"

I thought Mom was going to have a coronary right there. "Cheryl! You don't have to give us a direct quote!" she said.

133

"Mama, I've never even *met* that girl! She didn't have the slightest idea who I was!" Cheryl retorted. "Oops. There goes Debbie's milk again." Cheryl jumped up and ran into the kitchen for a towel. I don't think we ever got through a meal without Debbie dumping her milk.

"I know it's not easy for you kids." Mom said. "People watch everything you do, and it's hard to measure up to their expectations."

"It's not just hard, it's impossible!" Cheryl retorted.

"It's bad enough when kids treat you that way, but grown-ups can be worse!" Linda added.

"I'll say!" Cheryl put in. "Remember when I was a freshman and I went away to that Episcopal boarding school in Wisconsin?"

Cheryl thought it was a great school. She loved the nuns, and most of the kids were friendly. The freshmen weren't allowed off the campus without a nun to escort them, and wherever they went, they were always in uniform. They wore wool skirts, blazers, hats, gloves—the whole works.

One day Cheryl and her roommates were walking along the sidewalk in front of the school, and a woman approached them. Looking directly at Cheryl, she asked, "Do you know the Rogers girl?"

Cheryl said yes, and then the woman said, "Well, she was here at a party on New Year's Eve, and she was drunk!"

One of Cheryl's roommates told the woman that Cheryl had been out of town over the holidays.

"Oh, you girls always stick together, don't you?" the woman retorted. Cheryl asked her what the "Rogers girl" looked like. "Well, she's about 5'6" and she's got long, straight, bleached-blonde hair," the woman replied.

"Well, I'm in her class," Cheryl said, "and she's no

taller than I am. Her hair is curly and short like mine, and she's a brunette like me. You must have confused her with someone else!"

"Nope," the woman insisted. "I was at a party and she was there and she was drunk!"

When Cheryl finished her story, we all just sat there for a minute. "Why didn't you just tell her who you were, Cheryl?" Linda asked.

"Because she wouldn't have believed me anyway. She wanted to believe that Roy Rogers' daughter was a bleached-blonde lush. I could have had every one of the nuns attest to my innocence, and it wouldn't have made a shred of difference to that woman. She'd already made up her mind. People believe what they want to believe, whether it's true or not."

But strangers weren't the only ones who could be unkind. As careful as Mom was about the people she hired to care for us, one time she made a mistake. After Pearl left and before Granny Minor came, Mom hired a little slip of a woman to be our nurse. Because this woman was a Christian, Mom thought her faith would be a positive influence on us.

But in spite of her religious beliefs, we all thought this nurse was mean. She didn't like Mimi at all, and Linda and I were obviously her favorites. That was because we were Roy Rogers's "only *real* children," as she put it. I guess the rest of us were not "real."

This woman used to make us pray a lot—not just during devotions. One time she drove us to the movies, and she made us kneel in the backseat all the way to the theater. We all had to thank God that we were able to go to the movies and that we were lucky enough to be living with Roy Rogers and Dale Evans. It wasn't that we were supposed to thank God for parents who loved us, but

135

rather, because such famous people would take us in.

One day, the nurse was especially cross with Mimi, and Cheryl made her back down. The nurse hit Mimi with a ballet slipper. It might seem as though a slipper wouldn't hurt, but the wood in the toe left a mark. When that happened, Cheryl saw red. She ran over and grabbed the slipper out of the nurse's hand, saying, "Mimi hasn't done anything wrong, and if you ever hit her again, I'll *kill* you!"

As soon as Cheryl told Mom about the incident, the nurse was given her notice. Mom and Dad were horrified when they realized the pressures this woman had placed on us. They never expected us to live up to those kinds of demands.

"You are more important to us than what other people think," Mom often told us. Because of the pain of her early years in show business, she was especially aware of the temptation of trying to live a life that pleased only the public. One night she shared those feelings with us.

"It was terrible for Tom when he was a little boy, before your daddy and I were married." Mom shook her head sadly. "When I came to Hollywood, my agent said I couldn't tell anybody I had a boy Tom's age. My contract would be cancelled. So I had to pass Tommy off as my brother when I introduced him."

"But Art Rush is a Christian!" Mimi protested. "Why would he encourage you to lie like that?"

"Art wasn't my agent then—he was Dad's. And I wasn't a Christian then, either. But it broke my heart to do it, and I know now that I shouldn't have. But I kept telling myself it would help pay for Tom's education. That wasn't true either—I wanted to prove something. So I asked him if he minded.

"Tom said just what you might think. He said, 'Mom, you do what you have to do, but don't ever ask me to lie for you. If you have people at the house, I'll just leave.' And that's the way it was, for several years."

Grandma Smith had taken care of Tom during his formative years, and she helped him to understand what it means to live for Jesus. He became a Christian as a young child, and he didn't live with Mom permanently until he was 12 years old. Some time later, when Tom was drafted into the Army, the news that Dale Evans had a grown son hit the newspapers. Mom was relieved to be free of that awful lie. She had paid a dear price for it.

It hurts a mother when her child hurts, and Mom knew that Tommy was deeply wounded by her choice. Her grief over Tom's painful childhood never went away completely. Although part of the reason Mom had made her choices to work was because of the necessity of earning a living, she continued to feel bad about it. Tom forgave her long ago, and although she has also forgiven herself, to this day she has never forgotten the painful consequences of putting her career ahead of Tom.

Because Tom had become a Christian while growing up, he continued to share Christ with Mom, and later, with Dad. When she married Dad, Mom made her own commitment to Christ.

"When I gave my life to Christ," Mom says, "I asked one thing of Him. I asked Him to let me live long enough to see each of my children accept Him as Saviour. If you don't have Jesus, you don't have anything."

Because Mom and Dad were concerned about our spiritual welfare, they wanted us to understand the difference between living to please God and living up to an unrealistic public image.

"Remember," Mom would say, "your life is the only Bible some people will ever read. What really matters is that you live lives that honor God."

"Yeah," I said one time, "but sometimes, kids of famous people are real jerks."

"That doesn't mean *you* have to be one," Dad said.

"It's always hard for the kids of famous people—or people who aren't famous but are in the public view, like missionaries and ministers," Mom added. "You're right, Dusty, some of them are real stinkers. I think they make unhappy choices, and sometimes they even ruin their lives because they can't stand the pressures. Daddy and I don't want you to make those kinds of choices, even though it's hard."

"It's not fair though," Cheryl protested. "Some people don't like your choices even when they *are* good. They think we have to be just like you and Dad."

"No, it isn't fair," Mom agreed. "People don't mean to be hard on you, but I know they are. It's important for you to be yourself, Cheryl." Then she turned to me. "Dusty, you can't be like your father. There is one Roy Rogers, and there is one Dusty, and I'm glad. There's only one of you—each of you is different."

"Yes, Mama, we know," Mimi said. "It just makes us mad sometimes, that's all. Oh, Sandy, you ate the last of the potatoes again! By the way, Mama, you have to drive me over to the library."

Mom sat there for a few seconds, and then she looked at Dad. He raised his eyebrows a little, but he didn't say anything.

"Things have changed a little since you were little. I'm as busy as I ever was, but now it seems like I'm always on the run. You all expect me to cart you around at your convenience, and I scarcely have time to breathe!"

"But that's what you're *supposed* to do," Mimi said.

"Who says so? With seven of you to keep track of, I'm running all the time. It's exhausting," Mom countered.

"I've had a little chat with Mama," Dad put in. "And I told her that I'm going to be here long after all of you are married and on your own. I want her to get some rest and to spend a little time relaxing with me! You girls are big enough to get around on your own. You can't expect Mama to be your taxicab any more."

"It's bad enough that you have to live in a fishbowl," Mom added. "I'm not willing for you to be spoiled on top of it!"

That ended the discussion. It wasn't as though the girls couldn't get around; they had all learned to drive on old Nelly Bell, the jeep from Dad's television series. And Cheryl used the money she'd earned from television commercials and from our summer tours to buy her own car.

If the big girls were having their problems, Sandy and I weren't faring much better. I was five months older than Sandy, but I was two grades ahead of him in school. Because he was having so much trouble with his learning disabilities, Mom sent him to the Mariane Frostig Remedial School. I ended up at Chatsworth Elementary.

Like the girls, I heard kids saying unkind things, and my solution was to withdraw. At school I became my own best friend. When you are your own best buddy, you learn to entertain yourself and to be creative. I don't remember feeling lonely, but I did spend a lot of time alone.

While Sandy played with his army men and read books about the Civil War, I built models, and I could be happy sitting out on one of the rocks at the ranch. After Dad gave me my first gun, I spent hours hunting squirrels and birds. I found a lot of contentment in just being alone with myself.

At school the other boys didn't want me on their teams for dodge ball, kick ball and other sports like that. I never really understood why, but I suspected it had to do with my being Roy Rogers, Jr. Because the other boys wouldn't play with me, I played jump rope with the girls, or I played tetherball. I used to beat the heck out of that thing.

I was glad when we could all be home at the same time, especially on birthdays and holidays. The time around Halloween was especially fun because my birthday came on the 28th. Mom's birthday is Halloween, and Dad's birthday is the fifth of November, so we had nine days of celebration.

Mom always fixed fried chicken and mashed potatoes for my birthday, and she made her own special cornbread in a skillet. She never bought our birthday cakes at a store—they were always homemade from scratch, and hand decorated. If she absolutely couldn't be home to make the cake herself, Leola made it.

Mom and Dad were never big on parties, but for my second birthday, they put on a large one. It was my first birthday after they were married, and maybe Mom wanted it to be extra special. I wore a little purple western suit—which I still have—and Edgar Bergen and Charlie McCarthy entertained us. Kathy Lee Crosby and Candice Bergen were there, along with Art and Mary Jo Rush's kids. When it came time for the cake, I dove into it with both hands!

As we got older and could make decisions about what we'd like to do, Mom let us choose the way we were going to celebrate. It was always a family thing—a barbecue in the backyard, or a trip to Griffith Park in Glendale, where we'd spend the day at the zoo. They had the best merry-go-round in the world there.

For Mom's birthday Dad always took us over to the drug store where we would buy her a pretty card and some little gift, and we'd dress up and go trick-or-treating. We knew everyone in our neighborhood, so we felt safe going door-to-door. Some people served us hot apple cider or popcorn, and then we came home with our loot.

Dad never wanted birthday cake on his birthday, so Mom always made him a butterscotch pie. He loves gadgets and unusual toys, so that's what we've always given him. One time I bought him an executive fly swatter that looked like a gun. He thought it was great!

Another time Cheryl found him a strolling bowling game. When you pull on a little handle, the pins stand up. The little bowling ball has feet on it. When the toy has been wound up, the ball strolls down the little alley and knocks the pins over. Every time anybody came over to the house for the first few weeks after his birthday, Dad had to show off his toy. It's in his museum today.

Autumn gave way to Thanksgiving, and we always had a big family celebration. Everybody had to come. Tom and his wife Barbara came down from northern California with their children, close friends of my parents came, and of course my grandparents came.

When Mammy Slye was older, her leg gave her too much trouble, and so a few times we went to their place. But most of the time Thanksgiving was at our house. We'd set up big tables all over the lawn, and Mom would cook turkeys and hams. Everyone would bring something, and we'd feast for hours.

With so much food, there would be leftovers for a day or two. Although everyone else called her the Queen of the West, we used to call Mom the Queen of the Leftovers because she never let anything go to waste. Of course there was never much danger of that with Sandy around.

One time Dad decided to invite Gabby Hayes over to join us a few days after Thanksgiving. Gabby's wife had recently died, and they had no children, so Dad thought it would be a good idea for him to be with us.

"Gabby says he doesn't feel up to coming," Mom said as she put the telephone receiver back in its cradle.

"Well," Dad grunted as he pulled on his boots, "we'll see about that. I'm going to drive over and see if I can talk him into coming. We'll stop off and do a little shooting if I can talk him into it."

Sandy and I hoped Dad would be able to bring Gabby back with him. We all liked him. Gabby was tall and striking when he was dressed up. With his hair and his beard combed, and his dentures in his mouth, he resembled the fine, polished Shakespearean actor he really was. But when he slipped his old rumpled hat on and took his teeth out, he became Dad's old sidekick—a different character altogether.

With us, he was always gentle and kind and friendly. He loved to tease Mom. "Come on, Butter Butt," he'd say to her. "Give us a hug!"

I don't think she was too surprised when he came in with Dad later that afternoon. They'd done some shooting, and Gabby was perky and full of fun. He wrestled around with Sandy and me for a little while, and then we sat down to dinner.

As usual, once grace was said the table was chaotic. Sandy, Mimi and I were all fighting over the potatoes, Debbie dumped her milk, and everyone was talking at once. Suddenly we realized that Gabby was sitting there sobbing. Tears were streaming down his face.

"Gabby, honey. What's the matter?" Mom got up and went over to him, putting her arm around his shoulder.

"You okay, Pappy?" Dad asked, his face creased with worry.

"You don't realize how lucky you are, Buck," Gabby said.

"What do you mean?" Dad asked.

"You know, Mom and I never had any kids. Just *look* at this beautiful family of yours."

None of us ever forgot that day. I don't think my dad ever had a friend who meant more to him than Gabby did. Not long ago Dad, Mom and I were making a record album together at the old Capitol Records building in downtown Hollywood. At lunchtime we headed out for a bite to eat.

Gabby's star is on the sidewalk right in front of the recording studio, and Dad paused there for a few moments, lost in thought. Suddenly he looked up and saw me standing there.

"We made more than 60 pictures together, old Gabby and me," Dad said. "He was probably one of the main reasons I became number one in the box office. He taught me so much. People loved Gabby—they loved us together.

"I'm so thankful, Dusty, that he was my friend. He was a good friend. He was my father, my brother, my buddy and my pal, all rolled into one." Dad's eyes misted. "There isn't a day goes by that I don't think of my old friend, not a day."

eleven

My sixth grade teacher looked like a Russian Bolshevik. She stood out because she weighed about 250 pounds, and she had the hairiest lip I've ever seen. She was as nasty as they come, and she wasn't impressed at all that I was Roy Rogers, Jr. Never once did she let me get my own way. She helped me learn to develop self-discipline by making me do things I didn't want to do.

For Christmas she decided that all of us should make angels for our mothers, and I dawdled my time away because I didn't want to do it. One day, just before Christmas vacation, Mrs. Burke kept me in from recess.

"You know something, Dusty?" she began. "I really don't care if you finish your project or not. It doesn't bother me. But your mom is going to be very disappointed. All the other mothers will have a beautiful angel; your mom will just sit in the corner and cry!"

145

It had never occurred to me that my mom would want something I made, even though she always fussed over everything I brought home from school. I kept thinking of Mom sitting in a corner and crying, and I finished that angel in two days! I felt good about my present for Mom. I wrapped it in white tissue paper at school and hid it under my bed when I got home.

Christmas vacation! What kid doesn't like it? For us, it meant a long and joyful celebration, beginning with the selection of our tree. That was a production in itself.

There was no way to put our entire family *and* a Christmas tree into the station wagon, so we took two cars and headed out to our favorite tree lot in the San Fernando Valley. With nine of us, there were always at least nine opinions about what kind of tree we should have.

"Are we gonna get a tall tree this year, Daddy?" Sandy asked.

"I think we should have it flocked, so it looks like snow!" Mimi suggested.

"It should be pink!" Dodie added.

"Yuck!" I moaned. "Pink is for girls!"

"Can we get a blue spruce this year, Dad?" Mimi threw in.

In Mom's car the conversation was probably much the same. To flock or not to flock, tall or short—those were the questions. Every year we did it differently from the year before, so we all got our chance to have it our way.

The scene at the tree lot must have resembled a Keystone Cops film. Sandy and I went in one direction, Dodie and Debbie in another. Debbie was the extrovert, always seeking new adventures, and Dodie tagged along behind her. The older girls all went their separate ways, too.

"Look here!" Cheryl called. "I found one!"

"So have I!" Mimi called.

146

"Keep shouting! We'll find you!" Mom hollered. We looked at plenty of trees, and then Dad spotted the biggest, fullest tree we had ever seen.

"Oh, Roy, that's too tall!" Mom said.

"Nah. The ceiling in the den is 14 feet. It'll fit."

"Look how full it is!" Linda added.

"I've never seen one that full," Mom mused. "I wonder why it's . . . "

"It's pretty! Let's have it flocked!" Mimi said.

"We can put red balls and red ribbons on it," Linda suggested.

"No, let's leave it green and put gold balls and gold ribbons on it," Cheryl put in.

"Well, are we all agreed that this is the tree?" Dad shouted above the argument. When we all shouted our approval, Dad bought the tree and tied it on top of the car. We decided to leave it green.

At home Dad dragged the tree off the car and took it in the house. That's when we found out why the tree was so full. The owner of the tree lot had drilled holes in the trunk of the tree and stuck branches in to make it full. When Dad dragged it into the house, all of the branches fell out!

Mom put Christmas music on the record player, and I made a big bowl of my famous popcorn while Dad struggled with the lights. Those were the days when, if one bulb burned out, the whole string went out, and each bulb had to be tested separately. It always seemed that the tree lights took the longest time to do, and if anything could ruin the holidays, I think it would have to be those lights!

We spent the evening decorating the tree and sharing memories of Christmas-past.

"Remember the tree we had in Hollywood Hills?" Cheryl asked. "You knocked it over, Dusty."

"I did not!" I protested.

We had the tree up in the family room that year. Joaquin and Lana loved to come inside and be with us. I went downstairs early one morning before anyone else was up. It was a day or two before Christmas. I opened the door and Joaquin tore in. He started skidding across the tile floor, slid onto the Navajo rug and kept on sliding until he hit the tree.

The whole tree came crashing down! You could hear it all over the house, and it woke everybody up. Dad jumped out of bed and tore downstairs with the rest of the family hot on his trail.

Dad was so mad he started yelling at Joaquin. "Get out of here you fool dog before I kick you all the way to Ohio!" Dad grabbed a newspaper to spank Joaquin, and chased him outside, still yelling.

"A little while later you came limping back into the house, sputtering and mumbling a whole string of naughty words," Cheryl reminded him.

"Well," Daddy explained, "I was barefooted, and the ground was covered with rocks and pebbles. I was so mad, I didn't notice, at first—but then I started to feel the pain! I could have wrung your neck, Dusty!"

We all laughed, and then Sandy said, "You were sure lucky to have a Christmas tree. I never had one 'til Mama and Daddy brought me here."

"No tree, Sandy? That's awful!" Linda was horrified. "But you did get presents, didn't you?"

"We always got a fresh box of cereal that hadn't been opened yet. Usually there was a prize inside, like you get with Cracker Jack."

"That's all? A box of cereal and a little prize?" Mimi said. "We got more than that in the orphanage. We used to get presents, and an orange, too!"

The first year Mimi lived with us, all she wanted was a

bag of oranges. She couldn't believe it when she saw the oranges on the ground under the trees outside. Mom saw to it that Mimi got oranges for Christmas every year after that.

The year Debbie came we had a real adventure that could have been a tragedy. The week after Christmas, Dad was out of town hunting ducks. One night Mimi stayed up late, and she was the last one to go to bed. Although she checked the doors and turned out the lights, she overlooked a candle that was burning on the television.

The candle burned down and caught the ribbons and other decorations on fire, which then melted the television set. It wasn't a big flame fire, but a slow, smoldering one that worked its way across the carpet and started on the piano. Cheryl and Mimi were sleeping in the room directly adjacent to the den, but the wall between the two rooms was made of stone, and they didn't smell the smoke.

It was Betty who woke up and smelled the smoke. Frantic, she called Cheryl and Mimi on the intercom.

"Cheryl! Marion! Wake up! The house is afire!"

"Don't panic, Betty," Cheryl said. "Did you wake Mom?"

"No! She'll get all upset! Oh, Cheryl!" Betty screamed.

"Be quiet!" Cheryl hissed. "Call the fire department and I'll get everybody up!"

When Cheryl called Mom over the intercom, Mom thought Cheryl was getting her up to drive us all to school. But the whole house was filled with cherrywood and redwood smoke. As soon as Mom realized what was happening, she was terrified. She had no idea where the fire was, and she didn't know how she was going to get all seven of us out.

Mimi and Cheryl woke Linda up, and they got the little girls out while Mom hollered for James. James woke Sandy and me up, and we all ran outside in our pajamas. Outside, Mom asked James where the fire extinguisher was, and he started jumping up and down and rattling off a string of sentences in Filipino. Suddenly he took off, running, and soon returned with the fire extinguisher.

James and I went back into the den and tried to get the fire extinguisher going, and I stepped on a hot coal. In the meantime, we could hear the sirens. The engines were going up and down the street looking for us. Betty had given them an address that didn't exist!

All she had to do was tell them we were right next to the cemetery, but not Betty! She would never admit to living next to "dead people." She wouldn't even go down to the mail box because it was too close to the cemetery!

Cheryl, Mimi and Linda, still in their pajamas, climbed into the jeep and drove down to the gate to find the fire department. When they finally arrived, they didn't even check to see if the front door was unlocked. They simply chopped their way in with an ax! By the time they put the fire out, there was serious smoke damage everywhere.

Mom and Dad had to replace the television and the piano, the front door, and the carpet in the den, the dining room, and in Sandy's and my room. The entire house had to be repainted.

That was quite a Christmas. It almost never snows in Chatsworth, but that year it did. Debbie's eyes were like saucers. I don't think she had seen snow since she left Korea, and these snowflakes were as big as silver dollars.

"It's not fair!" Debbie protested when we reminded her of it. "I don't remember it. Wouldn't it be fun if it snowed this year?"

"I had all the snow I ever wanted to see when I grew

up in Ohio," Dad said. "I've been out here so long that my blood's too thin!"

"Tell us about your Christmas, Daddy, when you were little." Debbie went over to where Dad was sitting and began to muss his hair. Playfully he pretended to bite at her hand. She squealed and jumped back, laughing.

"Well, li'l darlin', when I was your age, all I got for Christmas was an orange, like Mimi, and an apple and a pocket knife. It's all my parents could afford."

"Poor Daddy!" Debbie stroked his face.

"Oh, Honey, in those days, Christmas wasn't like it is today. 'Most everyone was poor, and we didn't think about lots of presents. Sometimes today we get so caught up in all the presents that we forget about the little baby in the manger, who only had straw to sleep on."

"But didn't Santa Claus bring you any toys?"

Dad coughed a bit and looked at Mom.

"Speaking of Santa Claus," Mom said, "guess what? Daddy talked with him today—all the way to the North Pole!"

"Did you Daddy?" Dodie's eyes widened.

"Yep, I did. And he said, 'Well, hello there, Roy. How are you?' And I said, 'Pretty good, Santa. I want to thank you for that pocket knife you gave me when I was a little boy. It helped me learn how to whittle!' And then Santa said, 'You're welcome! What can I do for you?'"

Debbie and Dodie were amazed. Daddy had actually talked with Santa Claus!

"Well, we talked back and forth like that for a little while, and then I said, 'Santa, do you know that Christmas is on a Sunday this year? I was wondering—do you suppose you could come by earlier on Christmas Eve—in the afternoon sometime? Christmas morning's pretty busy, and we don't want to miss church.'"

151

"What did he say?" Sandy shouted.

"He said he would! Now let Mama read us the Christmas story from the Bible, and then it's time for bed."

When Christmas Eve came, we were all excited. The little girls wondered if we'd get to watch Santa Claus put our presents under the tree. Debbie spilled her milk twice at lunch, and Dodie could hardly eat. Then Mom laid it on us. Due to all of the excitement, and because we were going to stay up late (and it was the only way she could figure out how to get the presents under the tree), everyone had to take a nap!

Sandy and I looked at each other and nodded. The same thing had happened a couple of years earlier. We'd gone, protesting, to our rooms, which were right off the den. We could hear Dad and Mom talking to each other and putting out all the presents. Santa was a myth! But we never breathed a word of it to Debbie and Dodie.

When it was time, Mom and Dad called us out. I don't think Sandy ever got over his astonishment at receiving presents on Christmas. It never mattered to him what we got. No one was ever more wide-eyed or thrilled with Christmas than my brother was.

One Christmas, Dad bought us a gas-powered go-cart with two engines. It was probably the most expensive toy he ever bought us. He picked it up about two weeks early and hid it in the barn. He rode it around every day "just to test it out." Sandy and I found it and rode around on it whenever he wasn't home. He had no idea we knew about it.

By Christmas afternoon the novelty had worn off, so Sandy and I crawled into the big boxes from Christmas and began rolling around on the lawn. Dad came outdoors to see what we were up to, and he started jumping up and down and waving his arms at us.

"You kids! What's the matter with you? I buy you this beautiful go-cart and what are you doing? You're out here playing with a bunch of cardboard. Next year all you're getting is the boxes!"

Whether we opened our gifts on Christmas Eve or Christmas morning, Christmas afternoon meant more presents from friends and family who came to visit. Mom sat near us with a notebook and a pen, faithfully recording every gift we received. During the next two weeks, we wrote thank-you notes to everyone who remembered us.

Because there were so many toys, many items were boxed up and given to orphanages and children's hospitals. I don't think it bothered any of us, though. Because of Robin, we understood that children who are ill need extra cheering up during the holidays. Sandy and Mimi had shared enough about life in an orphanage that we had developed a strong sense of compassion for impoverished children who have no one to love them.

During the weeks between Christmas and New Year's we enjoyed our time at home. The girls were dating by that time, and Sandy and I loved to tease them— especially Cheryl. Sometimes they'd be in the den, playing pool with their dates, and Sandy and I would run in, screaming.

Other times we'd go outside and sit near the window. Every once in a while we'd raise up and put our noses on the window, making faces and staring at them. If they started kissing, we'd tap on the window.

"Two little lovers, sitting in a tree, K-I-S-S-I-N-G," we taunted. "First comes love, then comes marriage, then comes Queenie with a baby carriage."

"Prince! You and Sandy stop that!" Cheryl yelled. "Mama! Make Sandy and Prince go away. They're being jerks again!"

Mom would chase us away, and we'd go out and play army with our 10-cent army men. Mom had a big cowbell Dad had picked up at a rodeo, and when it was time to come in, she'd go out in the backyard and swing it as hard as she could. You could hear it all over the ranch.

Mom didn't need the cowbell, though. Her years in show business had served her well. She could project well enough to be heard even from the rocks high above the house. In later years she got a megaphone, and we could hear her from almost anywhere on the ranch: "Now hear this!" she yelled.

Before we knew it, Christmas vacation was over. New Year's Eve was Mom and Dad's anniversary, and since they were never the party type, we always celebrated at home with friends. I would pop the popcorn and we'd all sit around watching Dad's old movies. Although New Year's Eve belonged to us, it was never a late night because Mom and Dad were usually a part of the Tournament of Roses Parade in Pasadena the next morning.

Sometimes they rode Trigger and Buttermilk, other times they were featured on floats, and a couple of times they took their custom-made Bonneville. The hand-tooled leather interior had 339 silver dollars imbedded into the upholstery. Twenty-six miniature guns replaced the usual door knobs, wiper blades and ignition keys and other items inside and outside of the car. Dad used to use it in his parades and shows, but when vandalism began to ruin it, he put it in the museum where it could be protected.

Although it seems like Pasadena puts on her best weather every year for the parade, in truth it was often cold and rainy. To keep the flowers fresh, the floats were—and still are—built in large barns with no heat. One especially cold year, the float Mom and Dad were riding was huge, and they were to sit high up top, riding on horses made of flowers. They never rode prettier horses.

Mom and Dad had to be in place on the float before the flowers were put on, so they arrived at the building at four in the morning. A cherry picker lifted them to their places on the bare frames of the horses. Once settled, they could not get down.

For three hours they sat in that cold building while volunteers decorated the horses. Every once in a while someone took pity on my freezing parents and came up in the cherry picker to bring them a cup of steaming coffee.

Just before it was time to move the float into position in line for the parade, that coffee hit my dad's kidneys.

"Dale!" he hissed. "I've got to get down. I have to use the rest room."

"Oh, Honey, you can't! You'll crush the flowers on the horse!"

"But I've got 20 cups of coffee to get rid of!"

One of the people who was working on the float overheard them. "I'm sorry, Roy," the worker said, "but there's no way to get you down without messing up that horse. We don't have the time or the flowers to redo it. Mrs. Rogers, you'll have to hand me your coat now. No one will see your costume if you wear it."

Dad looked at Mom. "I do't know, Mama," he said. "I don't know what I'm gonna do."

"Try to think of something else!" Mom suggested as she reluctantly parted with her coat.

The parade started and Mom kept looking at Dad. She could tell he was uncomfortable. The rain had begun to fall softly when they were inside, but now it was coming down hard. Dad gave Mom another miserable glance.

"Just smile and wave!" she said.

They rode on for 15 minutes or so, and then Mom glanced over at Dad again. He was grinning, and steam was rising up from where he was sitting.

"Roy!" she said. "You didn't!"

"Well, what the heck!" he answered. "It's pouring down rain and I'm already soaking wet. Nobody will ever know the difference!"

That year the rain served a useful purpose, but most of the time it was a nuisance. Rain is especially hard on silver, and Dad didn't like to take his silver saddles out in it. One year he decided he didn't want to do it again. He phoned a saddle maker in Wyoming and ordered a plastic yellow saddle, decorated with red roses especially for the parade. That New Year's morning dawned bright and sunny—the best weather Pasadena had seen in years!

Winter gave way to spring, and like Christmas and New Year's, Easter was a major event for our family. Mom and Dad were usually part of the sunrise services at the Hollywood Bowl, so they got up early and went there. Granny Minor made sure we were all ready for church when they got back.

We always had new Easter outfits, and the girls had fancy hats to wear. Every year the magazine photographers arrived bright and early to take our pictures.

"Okay now, Dusty," Mom would say, "you grab Sandy's hand there. Dodie and Debbie, you too. Cheryl, fix Dodie's hat, will you please?"

"Can't we go hunt for eggs?" I asked.

"As soon as we get our pictures taken, Dusty," Dad answered.

We'd line up and walk down the driveway, and the photographers would shoot away. Then they followed us around when we looked for the eggs. That was a mad scramble! We really battled it out to see who would get the most.

Dad raised rabbits, and one year he decided to let a

bunch of little rabbits loose. It was a zoo! All seven of us were running around, screaming like Comanches and falling all over the place as we tried to catch the bunnies. Rabbits run in circles when they're scared, so the rabbits were all running in circles and we were running in circles and the photographers were running in circles behind us. It was great fun.

We spent the rest of the day relaxing and eating jelly beans and Easter eggs. By afternoon Mom and Dad were ready for naps, so it was a lazy day. We always enjoyed it.

Spring goes quickly, I think, and before long, June was upon us. As hard as Mrs. Burke worked with me, by the end of the school year she decided I just wasn't ready for junior high school.

"I think Dusty needs an extra year to mature, Mrs. Rogers," she told my mother. "I'd like to keep him back. I think it would be best for him in the long run." So I spent another year in the sixth grade. Then Mom and Dad decided that Sandy and I were ready for another go at military school.

Mom on the set of the TV Show.

Pat Brady and Nellybelle.

twelve

At first Sandy and I were apprehensive about going back to military school. Mom explained that the school was in Woodland Hills—close enough for us to come home every day. Dad's director, Bill Witney, was sending his son John there, too.

Ridgewood Military Academy was a school for boys from first through ninth grade. The well-kept buildings were inviting, and the lawns and hedges were perfectly manicured. Palm trees and oaks and other greenery gave the school a warm and friendly look. Parents were always welcome, which made Sandy and me glad.

Colonel Metcalf, the Commandant, was a friendly man with glasses and a ready smile. His wife was the office secretary, and everybody liked her. A married couple did all the cooking, and the food was good.

The teachers all believed in scholastic excellence, but

they also encouraged us to excell in athletics and to develop leadership qualities. By the time I graduated, I had advanced to the rank of major.

A lot of the boys stayed at Ridgewood throughout the week and went home on weekends. As good a school as it was, Sandy and I felt sad when we saw the little first and second graders away from home for such a long time. I didn't think it right for such little fellows to be away from home for a week at a time.

As I grew older and could assume more responsibility, I was in charge of some of the little guys. Sandy and I both tried to encourage them and to be like big brothers to them. More than once I told myself that when I grew up, I'd never send my children away to boarding school.

At Ridgewood I found it a bit easier to make friends. In seventh grade Pat Notaro, Keith Keener and I really liked each other, and we played football together. I made captain of the team, and in our final year we were five and one for the season.

But I didn't stop with football. I went out for basketball, volleyball, wrestling, baseball and track, as well, and Keith and Pat were on all the teams with me. We were also together on the yearbook staff. Keith was the editor-in-chief, Pat was the activities editor, and I was the art and advertising editor.

Keith and Pat were the leaders of our battalion, and during our last year, they were the commanders who led our battalion to a 99.9 percent on our annual inspection. The California Cadet Corps sponsored the inspection, which was conducted by a team from the National Guard.

During my last year in military school, we had a blue and gold military prom. Everyone had to come, and we all had to invite girls—no stags allowed. The academy had a deal with a local private girls' school, and for those of us who needed a date, one would be arranged.

I didn't know any girls except my sisters, so I filled out a questionnaire to help the girls' school arrange for my date. I had to tell my name and my age and my height, so I could be matched. When the girl was selected, I was given a phone number to call.

All of us lined up at the pay phone at school to make the dreaded telephone call. I was so bashful, it took a lot of prodding for me to pick up the phone. My date sounded really nice, which was a relief. I told her my mom and I would pick her up.

Mom made me buy her a corsage, and on the way to pick her up I sat in the back seat of the car wanting to die. We pulled up to the girl's house, I went up the walk and rang her bell. When the door opened, I just stood there.

My date didn't match me at all! She was at least a foot taller than me—she had to be seven feet tall! She had the biggest chest I'd ever seen, except for Leola, and her gown was low cut and strapless. I stood there holding that corsage, wondering where in the world I was supposed to pin it!

"Here!" I finally gasped, and I shoved the corsage into her hand. At the dance, I never danced once with her. She didn't suffer from it, though, because all the other guys wanted to dance with her. I spent most of the evening in the rest room.

I was so grateful for the weekend! I needed some time to run off steam and to enjoy being a boy. When Dad was home, Sandy and I could hunt on the ranch. But when Dad wasn't home, we weren't allowed to hunt because of the danger.

Dad had strong feelings about gun safety, and for that reason he hated BB guns. A lot of the other guys had them, and Sandy and I decided Dad was just being stubborn about it. One day I faked a note to the local toy store, saying it was all right for Sandy and me to buy ourselves BB guns.

After that our pals George and Elton White came over often with their guns, and we roamed the ranch, shooting at squirrels. Sandy always managed to get shot in the arm or the back at least once, but in spite of the pain and heedless of my Dad's warnings, we never once considered the danger.

One of the barns was a storage place for Dad's museum things. I went in and found a big case of old 78 records. There were records by the famous opera star Enrico Caruso and some by Guy Lombardo, as well as some of Dad's and the Sons of the Pioneers. I had no idea how valuable they were. I found a chipped record, and tossed it. The record sailed through the air like a condor. We took a whole box of them out into a pasture and let them sail, shooting at them. If Dad had ever found out, I'd have bit the dust right then.

Sandy and I liked target shooting with our BB guns. One day we bought a new supply of army men, and we went out into one of the fields to shoot them.

"Okay, Sandy," I said. "Let's line them up."

"Let's tie string around little pieces of wood and bury them in the dirt. Look!" Sandy worked feverishly with several pieces of wood and string. He buried them and set army men on top of the dirt, then backed away.

"Pow! Pow!" he yelled, making all kinds of explosion sounds. He jerked on the strings, and puffs of dirt flew up as the men toppled over.

Then we lined up the soldiers again, backed away and shot them down. So intent were we on our army maneuvers that we never noticed Debbie and Dodie, who had come to the pasture to see what we were doing.

I shot at one of the army men, and the BBs bounced off. Suddenly Debbie started screaming and jumping up and down, holding her face.

"Oh, no!" I yelled. "Debbie, what happened? Debbie! Debbie!" She just kept screaming and crying, and she wouldn't pull her hands down from her face.

"I'm gonna get Daddy!" Dodie cried, and took off down the pasture. "Daddy! Daddy! Dusty shot Debbie!"

Debbie finally calmed down enough to speak. "Dusty, you b-b-broke my tooth!" she sobbed.

Mom and Dad came running into the pasture. Mom was screaming Debbie's name, and Dad's face was drained of color. "Debbie!" he called. "Are you all right?" He grabbed her and checked her over carefully.

"She's okay, Mama. Broke her tooth, though," Dad said. Relief was written all over his face as he hugged her.

I expected both Mom and Dad to rage at me, and I knew I had it coming. I felt sick inside.

Dad stood up. "Dusty and Sandy, give me those guns," he said slowly. His voice was strangely calm. "Now come into the house."

We followed along. Dad told us to go to our rooms while he and Mom took Debbie to the dentist. Later on they called us into the den.

"Sit down here, boys," Mom said. "We want to talk to you."

"You know," Dad said, "I've taught you boys both about gun safety from the time you were little tykes. I've spoken about how dangerous BB guns are until I was blue in the face. And now, Dusty, *you have maimed your little sister for the rest of her life.*"

How those words cut me! I knew they were true, and I felt awful.

"That tooth you shot out," Mom said, "was Debbie's

permanent tooth. It can never be replaced. The dentist can cap it with an enamel one that will look almost real when she is older, but until she stops growing, she'll have to have a silver tooth right there in front.

"Sandy, you are just as responsible as Dusty is," she continued. "Every time Debbie smiles at you, you're going to have to live with the knowledge that you did it."

That was it. No anger. No punishment. They were both visibly upset, but there was no yelling, no lengthy lecture. I'd have felt much better with a whipping, but they were right. The consequences of feeling responsible every time Debbie smiled at me, or seeing that silver tooth in every picture of her after that, always tore me up.

Sandy and I tried hard the next few days to make it up to Debbie, and I think she enjoyed the extra attention, but she didn't seem to hold a grudge about it. She was such an extrovert and so friendly that she didn't let anything bother her much or interfere with making new friends and trying new things.

The older girls were making new friends and trying new things, too. It seemed like we never saw them much anymore. Kids never think time is passing quickly, but I'm certain Mom thought it was running away from her when all three of my big sisters decided to marry within a few months of each other.

She and Dad both thought they were too young, and urged them to finish college first, but young love is often impatient. It wasn't long before there were only four of us kids at home.

Sandy and I both had jobs in local supermarkets. I worked at Ralphs and Sandy worked at Hughes, because the stores all had policies against family members working together. One night at dinner we got to talking about the craziness at work, and laughing about the extra money we were making because of the extra hours we were putting in.

"You should see the people, Mom. They're buying everything in sight!" Sandy said. "I wonder if they're even looking at the labels!"

"At our store, too," I added. "All the canned goods are going fast—and bottled water, too."

"Well, son, people are a bit worried these days," Dad explained. "We just don't know how things are going to work out in Cuba; Kennedy's made a strong stand. We just can't have those missiles aimed at our military bases here in the States."

"There's so much sabre rattling going on!" Mom said. "So much talk of war."

"In the Civil War they really did have sabres," Sandy put in. "I'm starting a collection!"

"Maybe we *should* have had a bomb shelter built on the property, Honey," Mom said.

Debbie started wriggling in her chair, and her eyes were getting wider and wider.

"Hush, now. Look at Debbie. You're scaring her!" Dad said.

Suddenly Debbie jumped up from the table and ran into the den, shouting, "No! No! I don't want a war! The guns are loud and people get hurt and there's nothing to eat and—" she began to sob. Dad hurried to comfort her.

Debbie had been so tiny when she came from Korea that we had no idea how much the war had etched itself on her mind. She was always so pleasant and happy, and she never talked about it, so we had thought she had no memory of the horrors of the first two-and-a-half years of her life.

As the missile crises settled down, Debbie was soon herself again. In the meantime, Sandy and I were ready for our own turns at learning to drive, and like the girls, we

165

had our first lessons on Nellybelle. That old jeep was a real family friend, all right.

Dad had a special reason for including her in the cast of his television program. During World War II, he had noticed that when children saw an army jeep coming down the road, they dropped everything and ran to the curb to watch it go by. They were fascinated with jeeps.

When the series went into production, and Pat Brady was chosen to be Dad's sidekick, Dad decided to put him in a jeep instead of on a horse. The jeep had to have some kind of personality, so Dad began with the name.

At that time, Howdy Doody and Buffalo Bob were very popular with the children all over the country, and Clara Bell the clown was Howdie Doody's sidekick. Nellybelle was a similar name with a funny ring to it, so Dad and Pat settled on that.

In order for the jeep to have a personality, she had to have a mind of her own. Dad had someone cut a slot just below the windshield, and a stuntman would lie across the front seat and drive her, looking through the slot so he could see where he was going. That way it looked as though she were driving herself. I can still see Pat Brady with his face all contorted, moaning, "Woah, Nellybelle!"

When the series ended in 1957, Dad brought her out to the ranch. She still wore her sign and bags on the side, and we all drove her everywhere. It didn't matter where we drove her on the ranch, she'd get stuck in places. A few times we rolled her over or got stuck up in the hills on large boulders, and Dad had to haul her out.

After Sandy and I learned to drive, Dad took her out to his other ranch in Thousand Oaks, where Trigger lived. Some of the men were using her to pull out an old tree stump, and the chain broke. Nellybelle lurched forward and hit the tree, totally demolishing her front end.

166

Every time we'd go out to the ranch to see Trigger, we'd see old Nellybelle lying there in a heap, rusting.

"Can't we fix her, Dad?" Sandy asked.

"Oh, Sandy, I don't think so. I don't think it's worth it. She's pretty well worn out."

One day some fans came out to the ranch to see Trigger, and Dad took them on a tour. One of them happened to own an auto body shop.

"Roy, that isn't Nellybelle!" he said.

"Yes, I'm afraid we had an accident. That's all that's left of her."

"Oh, I can't stand to see her like that!" he said. "Can I send my guys out to pick her up? Maybe we can do something with her."

Dad agreed, and a few days later a wrecker went out to Thousand Oaks and picked her up. Six weeks later they brought her back, all painted and dent-free. It was like having an old friend back. She's in the museum today, just like new.

After I learned how to drive on Nellybelle, I asked Dad if I could buy my own car. I'd graduated from the military academy and was getting ready to start school as a sophomore at Chatsworth High.

"Have you got one in mind?" he asked.

"Yeah. It's a nice one—a '56 Chevy.

"Do you have enough money?"

"Not really, Dad. I've been saving a bit from my job, and put together with what Mom has saved from the commercials and the summer shows, I have about half. But I have to start school in a few weeks, and I'd like to be able to drive myself.

"Half, huh?" Dad mused. "Well, I'll tell you what. I'll pay for half of it, and we'll cover your insurance. I'll give you enough money for one tank of gas each week, and if you have any mechanical problems, you take it over to that car dealership I own down on Ventura Blvd. We'll give you a discount. Any other expenses, you have to cover for yourself. It's the same rules I made for your sisters. Just be sure you live up to your reputation!"

"I'll try, Dad," I said. I knew he was referring to my being named "Most Reliable" at Ridgewood. "Thanks!"

A few weeks later it was time to start my sophomore year in high school. Chatsworth was a brand-new school with about 700 students. The year before, Dad had dedicated the school, and he told everyone I was coming.

"Next year my son will be coming here," he said. "He's 6'4" and weighs about 210 lbs., so he'll probably be on the football team."

When I drove into the parking lot that first day, there must have been 200 kids waiting there for me. I slipped in, driving my seven-year-old Chevy, and stood around with the rest of the kids for awhile. They didn't even know I'd shown up. That afternoon I told Mom about my day.

"The kids were all asking each other questions like, 'What does he look like?' 'Do you think he'll be wearing fancy clothes?' 'I'll bet he drives a Jaguar!'"

Mom just shook her head. She'd heard these stories hundreds of times. "Fat chance after what you did to *mine*!"

"Dad will never let me live that one down!" I chuckled. When I was first learning to drive, Mom let me drive her Jaguar up and down the driveway. One day she and Dad were both gone, and I decided to give it a try without their supervision. I was going up and down the driveway, hot-rodding it. I stepped on the gas, kicked it in gear and twisted the drive shaft. Dad grounded me for a month.

"What did you do in the parking lot today?" Mom asked. "Did you tell the kids who you are?"

168

"Naw. I just laughed! After school some guy followed me out to the parking lot. 'That your car?' he asked me. I said 'yeah.' 'Is that the best your dad could do for you? My dad's just a writer, and look at what I'm driving.'"

"What *was* he driving?" Mom asked, cocking her head a bit as she looked up at me.

"He was driving a brand new Thunderbird." I let out a low whistle. "Sure was classy!"

"What did you say to him?"

"I'll tell you. I said, 'Listen up. I bought mine with money I *earned*. Did you?'"

Mom just beamed. "Oh, Dusty, I'm so grateful! I'm proud of you!"

That made me feel great! I always felt taller when I knew my mom was proud of me. For the next few weeks the kids checked me out every day to see what I was wearing and how I combed my hair. It got to be a drag. But I didn't have any fancy clothes, and after awhile things settled down.

I joined the choir and took drama. Things were going pretty well, until one warm autumn day. That Friday, something happened, and it changed our lives forever. I was sitting in Spanish class, looking out the window. It was unseasonably warm, but the air was fresh. The sunlight cast a glare against the glass, and I wanted to be outside. Suddenly the loudspeaker interrupted the teacher.

"May I have your attention please," the principal was saying. "We have just received reports that President Kennedy was shot in Dallas, Texas just moments ago. We will keep you informed when we hear anything new."

I have never again experienced such sustained silence. I don't know how long we sat there before we began to look at each other. Some of the girls began to cry, softly. A few minutes later, the bell rang, and we filed out to the assembly area. We dreaded what we might be told.

"I'm very sorry," the principal said. "The President is dead."

Just like that. We wandered around from class to class, stunned into silence. The school was like a tomb for the rest of the day. Here and there you could hear muffled sobs and people sniffling. In class, some kids folded their arms on their desks, buried their heads and wept.

After school I drove home. The television was on, and everyone was crying. For the next four days the grief of the nation was the only thing on our minds. John Kennedy had captured the imagination of the nation's youth. We liked his vitality and his youthfulness, and I especially enjoyed his sense of humor. He had won people over.

The President's death ushered in a decade of tragedy for our nation. Other men would die at the hands of assassins, and great grief would govern the lives of many people. Racial unrest, the upheaval of human values, the terrible war in Viet Nam—all that lay ahead of us. But for my family, tragedy was about to take its toll much closer to home.

thirteen

Mom and Dad decided against a summer tour in 1964. They needed a rest, and they wanted to spend some time relaxing with Sandy and me and with the little girls—who were no longer very little. They decided on a vacation in Hawaii.

"Oh, this stiff neck of mine!" Dad groaned as he eased himself into a chair one afternoon. "It hasn't let up for days."

"You've had that pain in your neck for too long, Honey," Mom scolded. "I want you to see a doctor before we leave for Hawaii."

"Nah! I probably gave it a good jerk when I was out racing in the speedboat."

"Or on the motorcycle, or doing stunts, or any one of a thousand other things you've done these past 30 years. But how you did it isn't the problem. The problem is, you

171

certainly can't go on in pain like this."

"We'll see, Mama," Dad said. "It'll go away."

But the pain didn't go away. It worsened day by day, until Dad was in so much pain he could no longer stand it. He finally agreed to see a doctor.

The examination revealed that the fifth, sixth and seventh vertebrae were jammed together because the discs were worn. The only solution was surgery. Doctors at the UCLA Medical Center would take a bone from Dad's hip and use it to separate the vertebrae.

Dad urged Mom to take Sandy, the little girls, and me to Hawaii alone. He would stay home to rest and have the surgery when we returned, since we all needed that vacation. Mom agreed.

We loved Hawaii! The girls loved the water and the music, and it was like a dream for Sandy. Everywhere he looked, there were servicemen. "As soon as I'm old enough," he told me, "I'm going to enlist!"

"Really, Sandy?" I asked. "Which branch?"

"Oh, I don't know. In the army I guess. That's all I've ever wanted. Come on. I'll race you to the water!"

When we returned, Dad went to the hospital. The surgery seemed to last forever, and even though it went well, Debbie mooned around the house, worrying. Mom tried to reassure her, but about a week after the surgery, Dad started running a fever.

His pain level increased, and the doctors identified his problem as a severe staph infection in his hip. His condition worsened daily. For five weeks it was touch and go, and we didn't know if we were going to lose him. Finally, he seemed to stabilize, but his condition remained critical.

"Is Daddy going to be okay, Mama?" Debbie asked several times a day. "Will he be home soon? Can I go see him?"

172

"Honey, we just have to trust in Jesus," Mom would say. "It's going to be a little longer before we can bring him home. He's been so sick, it will take him some time to spring back. He needs to spend some time in the convalescent hospital because he's too weak to take care of himself here at home.

"I could take care of him," Debbie said.

Mom just hugged her. "Listen, Debbie Lee. I've been watching how grown-up you're getting to be. Almost 12! I want to have your picture taken. It won't do for you to look all worried in it, so you perk up!"

Debbie did perk up when she went to visit Dad, and he was always more cheerful after her visits. Although all of us responded to her warmth and affection, the magic between Dad and Debbie had never diminished.

One summer day just before her birthday, Debbie rushed into the house, dragging Dodie behind her. "Mom! Mom! Guess what?"

"A bunch of us from church are going to get to go to Tijuana next Monday," Dodie explained.

"We're going to take gifts to the children in the orphanage down there. Maybe we can take some flowers. I love flowers, don't you? Kathy and Joanne Russell are going. Isn't that neat? We can go, can't we, Mom?"

"I don't know, Honey," Mom said absently. "Dusty, did you and Sandy get that trash hauled out?"

"Yup."

"But Mom! You always let us choose the way we celebrate our birthdays," Debbie reminded her. "Since mine is that week, can't this be my present? Please?" Debbie grabbed Mom's hand dramatically and squeezed.

"Oh, all right! And I have good news, too. The doctor said that if your dad continues to improve, the doctor may take him off the critical list pretty soon!"

I knew that Mom was worried about Dad. The stresses of the past few weeks were beginning to take their toll. The following Sunday we went to church as usual. I sat with the high school kids, and Debbie sat in the choir. Dodie was with Mom. During the service, Dodie suddenly didn't feel well. At home, Mom put her to bed.

"I'm afraid your Tijuana trip is out," she told Debbie. "You may end up with this same bug! I think you'd better stay home. Cheer up, though, Honey. The doctor said we can move Daddy to the convalescent hospital tomorrow. He's doing better!"

Debbie was thrilled about Dad, but she was heartsick about the trip. She pleaded and begged, and Mom finally gave in. The next day Mom dropped Debbie off at the church before she drove to the convalescent hospital in Bel Air, where Dad had settled in at one that afternoon. Just off the critical list, he was still hooked up to IV bottles, and he was in a body cast.

Sandy and I spent part of the day at the church, and late that afternoon we headed home. When we went into the house, Granny Minor was on the telephone. As she spoke, I became aware of snatches of conversation.

" . . . try to keep it from the press . . . if Mr. Rogers hears it on the radio . . . yes, on the highway there between Oceanside and San Clemente . . . yes, it was terrible . . . little Joanne Russell, too . . . . The police said they would need someone to go down there and make a positive identification."

"What's wrong, Granny?" I asked when she had placed the receiver back on the telephone.

"Oh, Dusty. Sandy. I didn't hear you come in." Her eyes were all red, and she began to cry. "I have some terrible news. We just got word from the police." She started crying.

"Police?" I was puzzled. "What is it?"

"Your sister . . . Debbie . . . Debbie was killed today!"

Sandy and I just stood there. It didn't make sense. Sandy and I sat down, and a kind of hazy disbelief fell on us for a few minutes.

"Granny, how did it happen?" I asked. Sandy just sat there, shaking his head.

"The bus and a station wagon hit each other head on. They think the bus blew a tire and swerved into the oncoming traffic. Everyone in the car was killed, and little Joanne Russell and Debbie."

"What was that about identification?" I asked.

"They need someone to make a positive identification. They would prefer someone from the family, but . . . "

"I can go, Granny, I have my car. But where's Mom?"

"She left the hospital about 45 minutes ago. She's on her way home now. Oh, I hope this isn't on the radio. She always has that radio on. If she hears it . . . " Granny began to cry again.

Suddenly I felt a kind of warmth come over me. It was a hot summer day, and a warm breeze was blowing outside, but this was a different kind of warmth. It was like an anointing. Immediately I felt calm, peaceful—settled.

All right now, Dusty. You're it. Your mother is coming home, and your dad is not here for her. Don't get hysterical; don't get excited. Just be here for your mom.

"Granny, Mom has to be taken care of before anything else happens," I said. "Does Dad know?"

"No. We called Mr. Rush, and he called the hospital. They've disconnected the radio and television, and they aren't allowing any visitors or telephone calls until Mr. Rush arrives. I don't know what we're going to do about your mama."

"I'll take care of it, Granny."

175

Not long after that I heard Mom's car come whipping up in the driveway. Sandy and I went out to meet her. She hopped out of the car and called to us.

"Hi, boys! How are you?"

Sandy started crying, and all the color drained from her face.

"What's wrong? What's wrong?" she cried.

Just then Granny Minor came outside, and she was crying.

"Oh no!" Mom cried. "Is it Roy? Has something happened to Roy?"

"No, Dale," Granny said quietly. "It's Debbie."

Then all hell broke loose. Mom burst into tears and ran into the house. She collapsed against the window seat, and Sandy and I followed her.

"Why, God? Why did you do this to me again?" she cried out. "Why my baby again? Oh, Jesus, please, please help me!"

I sat down next to her, and I took her by the shoulders. She was crying so hard that I shook her a little to get her attention.

"Mom!" I said firmly. "Mom! For as long as I can remember, you've been telling me to trust Jesus. Now is the time for you to do that. Debbie is okay! She's with Him!" She nodded, and she put her head in my lap and cried. I held her for what seemed like hours. Finally, she grew quiet.

"Mom," I whispered, "what about Dad? You have to pull yourself together now. He's not strong enough to handle this. He's going to need you. And what about Dodie?"

"Oh, my God! That poor child!"

"She's in the backyard, Dale," Granny told her. Mom found Dodie sitting with the dogs, crying. They talked together for awhile, but I never learned what they said to

176

each other. They cried some more, and after they came in, Mom called the hospital.

"Well," she said after a while, "he knows. Art told him."

"Is he okay?" Granny Minor asked.

Mom shook her head. "Art said he went to pieces. 'Why her?' he kept asking. 'Why her?'" Mom started crying again. "Then he became so angry that he tore out all his IVs. Art and the nurses got him calmed down, and then he cried. He kept trying to get out of bed, and they finally put him under heavy sedation. They're afraid he'll tear up the repairs they've done. He's back in intensive care now. I'm going out to the hospital in a few minutes."

In a time like that, a certain numbness takes over, and it's hard to piece everything together later on. Most of the events of the hours that followed remain a blur to all of us. Bob Russell—Joanne's father—and their family doctor drove to San Diego and identified Debbie and Joanne at the coroner's office.

For Bob, the experience must have been shattering. The accident left both girls terribly mutilated. Apparently Debbie and Joanne had been standing near the front of the bus when the left front tire blew. Debbie went through the windshield and Joanne was jammed beneath the dashboard.

They were on a section of Interstate 5 that had come to be know as Slaughter Alley because of the outrageous number of traffic fatalities that occurred there week after week. It was several more years—and many more tragic deaths—before the State of California widened the two-lane highway and made it a safe thoroughfare.

Because Joanne's sister Kathy was severely injured in the accident, her family was with her at the hospital in Oceanside. Mom made the arrangements for a double

177

funeral at Forest Lawn, selecting both caskets and ordering all the flowers. A representative from Forest Lawn suggested the caskets remain closed. The coroner, he explained, had advised the caskets not be opened because the physical damage was so severe.

"Oh, please," she begged him, "do whatever you can so I can see her one last time. When our little Robin died, I refused to look at her in her casket, and I didn't let my other children see her. I've regretted that decision ever since. Please do what you can."

I believe it was the mercy of God that enabled the mortician to accomplish the monumental task Mom had asked of him. No one would ever have known how Debbie died. She was absolutely beautiful as she lay there, all dressed in pink and holding a little blue stuffed animal. She looked as though she were asleep. I couldn't help remembering the day she'd first come home to live with us, and how sweetly she slept on my bed, with the little beads of perspiration on her face.

I still hadn't cried, and although I gave every appearance of being calm on the outside, inside I struggled. "Lord," I prayed, "I know your timing is impeccable, but right now, it seems cruel. I can't understand why you would do this! We come from a good Christian family. We honor you with our thanks at every meal. We worship you every week in church. Debbie was serving you when she died. Look at what Mom and Dad have been going through these past two months. Why now?"

We lived as though we were in a dream for the next few days. It was as though God gave us all some kind of supernatural anesthetic that deadened the pain and enabled us to get through those first awful days. About a week after the accident, Mom went into Debbie's room to go through her things to prepare to give them away. It was too soon. Suddenly all the "novocain" wore off at once.

"Oh God!" she shouted. "I don't understand! It isn't fair! It isn't fair! What have I done? What have I done? What did she do? It isn't fair!"

My Grandma Smith had flown out from Texas to be with us, and she ran down the hall. "Frances!" she called out to my mom. "Frances! Where is your faith? I'm ashamed of you!"

"You don't understand!" Mom cried. "You can't understand. You've never lost a child. I've lost *two!*"

"Frances," Grandma answered gently. "Debbie used to love flowers. Remember how she used to pick bunches of them for me when I came to visit? God's garden is the world, and His children are His flowers. He has a large mansion with many rooms. Sometimes He wants flowers for His mansion. Sometimes He picks a full-grown rose, sometimes half-opened. Sometimes a bud. He's taken a bud. Doesn't He have the right? It's *His* bud."

That seemed to settle it for Mom, and though she mourned Debbie's death, she was able to work through her grief with a renewed sense of faith and purpose. As she had done when our little Robin died, she began to write a book. The royalties from *Dearest Debbie* were donated to World Vision International, and once again, God began to redeem the pain of our loss.

Dad remained in the hospital, in deeper despair than I'd ever imagined. Hoping the familiar surroundings of the ranch would help, the doctors allowed him to come home. Dad grieved a long time for Debbie, and more than once I wondered if he had lost his faith altogether.

It is true that Christians do not grieve in the same way unbelievers do, but pain is pain, and grieving is hard work. For the person in top physical condition, grief eats at the heart; for someone struggling to recover from serious ill-

179

ness and extensive surgery, it can be overwhelming.

Like us, Joanne Russell's family was hurting, too. Right after the funeral, Bob left home, and nobody knew where he was. His sons and I drove around town looking for him, and for a few days, Mrs. Russell thought he'd driven back East to be with some of his family. When that proved to be wrong, she filed a missing person's report.

About two weeks after the funeral, my friend George White came over for a visit. We were goofing around on the ranch, and we headed for one of the barns that nobody used. As we came close to the barn, I saw something shiny, and I realized it was a car. We walked toward it.

Suddenly George grabbed my arm. "Oh Dusty," he said, "don't go any closer."

It was Mr. Russell's car, and he was sitting in it, but it was obvious that he had been dead for some time. He'd left the window open, and flies and maggots were crawling all over him. His face had puffed up, and his skin had turned black. The coroner said he'd overdosed on sleeping pills. There was evidence of carbon monoxide poisoning, too.

For weeks I could not erase the image of that moment. I couldn't think, I couldn't eat—and I couldn't sleep. Whenever I closed my eyes, it was as though the picture had engraved itself permanently on my mind.

I began to wonder if I would ever be free of the memory—the image—that tortured me. It was as though the devil himself were using it to weaken my faith, and I began to think he was succeeding. At church we had a prayer meeting, and the people laid hands on me, praying for deliverance from the oppression I felt.

"Lord," I said, "you are the only One who can help me. Please, please take these images away from me, and heal me of this awful experience."

Again, a kind of warmth settled over me, and from that day on, I never again was troubled by the memory of Bob Russell's tragic death. I remember it vividly to this day, but the images no longer torture me.

At that same prayer meeting there was a young girl who suffered from convulsions. I was with her when the first one hit, and as she dropped to the floor, I could see that she was having trouble breathing. I knelt beside her and turned her head so she couldn't bite her tongue.

A seizure can be a frightening thing to witness, but for the person who experiences it, the emotional aftermath can be brutal. People tend to shun what they do not understand, mostly because of fear. But even though I'd never witnessed a seizure, I recognized it at once, and I didn't feel afraid.

When the little girl's seizure came to an end, I reassured her. Her epilepsy was severe, and for weeks after that her mother would call me to come and sit with the girl because she was asking for me. Each time there was a seizure, I prayed for healing and deliverance.

Today's she's a wife and a mother, and I like to think that God used me in her life. Through Robin and Sandy's problems, God had shown me how to exercise compassion and minister hope.

The combination of these events made me realize something Mom had been trying to teach us for as long as I could remember. There is more to being a Christian than merely living in a Christian home, saying grace and attending church.

I'd received Christ as my Saviour when I was eight or nine years old, and I'd made my own choice to be baptized. In the fall of 1963, I'd rededicated my life to God at a Billy Graham Crusade for Christ in Los Angeles. But I was becoming acutely aware that God was interested in an even more personal relationship. In the months that followed, God was about to sharpen that awareness in ways I could never have anticipated.

fourteen

By the fall of 1964, Dad had begun to pull out of his weakened physical condition, but Mom wasn't doing well. The shock of Debbie's death plunged her into diabetes which, the doctor told her, was not all that uncommon. With both Mom and Dad on a physical low, they were home most of the time.

Dad had bought some property out in the desert near Victorville, and for some time they had discussed a move. Now that the older girls were married, there were only three of us kids left at home. The rambling ranch in Chatsworth had become cumbersome. There was no need for nannies anymore, and Leola was gone.

I hated the idea of moving. I'd made good friends at Ridgewood, and now at Chatsworth I had been accepted as "one of the guys." Mr. Gustafson, my choir teacher, was helping me overcome my shyness. He seemed to care about me, and he'd encouraged me to sing a solo at one of the spring programs the year before.

One day one of the English teachers, Mr. Bradley, called me in to talk.

"Dusty," he said, "I want you in my speech class."

"Speech?" I asked. "There's nothing wrong with my speech!"

Mr. Bradley smiled and shook his head. "No, no, not that kind of speech. In my class you give talks. I give you a subject, you write a speech, and then you get up and speak to the class."

"You've got to be kidding! I'm not getting up in front of anyone!"

"I want you in there, Dusty."

So, I joined the speech class and the drama class, and Mr. Bradley spent a great deal of time working with me. We did a lot of plays at Chatsworth High, and one time I was especially eager for my folks to see me in *The Devil and Daniel Webster* because I was playing Webster. I was crushed when I found out they had to be out of town the weekend we were to perform.

"It's no problem, Dusty," Mr. Bradley said. "We can give a special performance, just for your folks! It'll be a dress rehearsal."

Everyone was thrilled to do a private showing for Roy Rogers and Dale Evans. Dodie came, too, and the three of them sat in the front row. We were all a bit nervous at the start, but then everything clicked. I think it was the best performance of the weekend. Mom just raved about us, and we all felt like award-winners.

A few days later Mom burst through the front door.

"Dusty!" she called. "Guess what? I was bragging about you this weekend. You have a wonderful talent!

Somebody told me that Youth for Christ is producing a film called *To Forgive a Thief*. It's about the half-way house program. I told them you'd love to try out for a part!"

I did want to try out. I enjoyed acting, and it sounded like fun. A few days later I received a call from a fellow from Youth for Christ. His name was Mel White.

"Would you be willing to read for a part in the film, Dusty?" he asked.

"Could you tell me about the part?" I asked.

"Sure. It's about a kid named Ted who gets a bad start. After he finishes his time with the Juvenile Authority, he's sent to a Christian half-way house. He's hostile and bitter, but the love of the Christians wins him over. We'd like you to try out for the lead."

"Boy! I'd love that!"

"Great. I'll send you the script, and we'll be out next week to have you read for the part. I have to be honest with you, though, Dusty. It's a toss between you and Gregory Peck's son."

Suddenly there were stars in my eyes. Even though it was a low-budget Christian film, for me it seemed like a major production. But when the script came, I panicked. I tend to procrastinate when I'm unsure of myself, and day after day I put off practicing the lines. Although I could have asked Mr. Bradley to help me, I kept postponing it until the morning of the reading.

Nervous, I poured over the script for a couple of hours. At the same time, the feeling of competition added to my stress, and my agitation produced a sense of defensiveness. By the time I did the reading, I was feeling aggressive and downright nasty—exactly what the part called for. And I got it!

We went into production and worked on location 18 hours a day for 11 days. Some scenes were shot in beautiful homes in the Rolling Hills Estates, and other times we went into some of the worst places in Los Angeles for barroom scenes.

I had to do a motorcycle jump scene although I'd never jumped a motorcycle in my life. I fell off and skinned my legs, but I had a great time. It never dawned on me that God had a purpose for me in playing the part of Ted until the day we shot a scene at the detention center in Chino.

They cleared a cell block for us, and I noticed a little boy. He couldn't have been more than nine years old. I turned to the deputy in disbelief.

"Why is he here?" I asked.

"Well, we don't have any place to send him right now."

"But why is he in jail? Why isn't he at juvenile hall or some place like that?"

"Because he's incorrigible. About four days ago he walked into his parents' bedroom, and while they were asleep he shot them both in the head with a .22. Murdered them."

I could hardly catch my breath. What had provoked such a terrible thing? Was he abused? Did they beat him? Had no one ever told him he was important? I looked into that sad, sad face, and I thought, *What would have happened if someone had reached out to this kid three weeks ago? What if someone had shaken his hand and said, "Hi there. How ya doing? Nice to see you. I appreciate you. You're a human being with worth and value. God loves you and I love you."*

I walked over to him and said, "Hi." I shook his hand, and he smiled. He seemed to be genuinely appreciative.

I'd walked into that cell block feeling like a big shot. Now, as the cell door closed behind me, I had a profound sense of purpose. *Remember, Dusty. Your life is the only Bible some people will ever read.* Mom's words suddenly

186

Dad and I at the Portland premiere of <u>To Forgive a Thief</u>.
(Courtesy of Ackroyd Photography Inc.)

took on new meaning, and I realized that even this low-budget, 29-minute film, starring a bunch of unknowns, could change the lives of a lot of people.

Dad and I flew to Portland for the premiere. It was the first time I saw it. When it was over, there was no applause—only silence. That warmth came over me again, and it seemed like God's hand rested on my shoulder. *I've given you that ball. Now Dusty, it's up to you to run with it.*

I looked at Dad, and his eyes were misty. People in the audience were crying, and I knew that God was going to use that ordinary piece of black and white film. During the next three years I took the film to almost 400 churches, encouraging Christians to support the half-way house program. To help young people instead of sticking them in jail. To help them feel loved and wanted. To bring them under the influence of the church. To reveal to them the love of God. To show that they are not alone, and that people do care.

As serious as I was about the ministry God had given me, I'm grateful for the example my mom set for me. I think she's the greatest Christian in the world, and if I ever wanted to know anything about living the Christian life, all I'd have to do is ask her.

But Mom is also a regular guy. She takes God very seriously, but she knows how to laugh at herself. She never makes the mistake of taking herself too seriously, and because of that, I knew it was all right to enjoy myself.

I was enjoying myself a lot at Chatsworth High. I'd had several girlfriends, each of whom took their turns caring for Peter Cottontail. Because I had finally gained some self-confidence and developed some warm friendships, it was all the harder to accept the fact that we were moving.

To avoid the problem of transferring in the middle of the term, I had to move out to Victorville a few months before we could move into our new home. Sandy was in a private school because of his learning disabilities, so I lived alone in a local motel and drove myself back and forth to school. I ate my suppers in the motel room because I didn't want to go out alone. It was probably the loneliest period in my life, and I was relieved when the rest of the family was able to move out to Apple Valley, just over the hill from Victorville.

At school, the teachers took a special interest in me. One was Mrs. Kurtz, my singing teacher. She spent a lot of individual time with me, and she encouraged me to join a barbershop quartet with David and Ron Powell and Dave Wallace. Those guys and I had a great time. We called ourselves the Fuzzy Wuzzies, and we sang every chance we could. We went to convalescent hospitals and churches—any place that would have us. Even I was surprised when I found myself playing the comic relief!

Mrs. Kurtz also encouraged me to join the Chamber Singers, an *a cappella* choir. I also joined the church choir, and I did a lot of singing and solo work. I enjoyed it.

Victor Valley had very little to offer in the way of entertainment in those days. The little desert community had one old hamburger joint, a drive-in, and one old theater that showed ancient movies. A lot of the time, we just cruised around in our cars. About the most exciting thing to do was to watch the Safeway trucks unload at 2:00 in the morning!

The church kids were shunned by the party-goers, and if you weren't part of one clique or the other, you were alone. The kids from my church had prayer meetings both on and off campus, and during lunch we went across the street from the school to a little hall, where we prayed together and goofed off. There was never any drinking or drugs with that group.

Sandy and I had both dated, and one day he came to me looking a bit sheepish. "Hey, Dusty. I gotta tell you something. I think Sharyn is about the nicest girl in the world."

"She is pretty neat," I said.

"She treats me so nice. She doesn't care about my problems with learning, you know? I love her a lot."

"You do? How do you know? You're only 17!"

"Well, I'll be 18 in June. Dusty, I'm gonna ask Mom and Dad to let me enlist."

"Sandy, you aren't even out of high school yet!" I protested.

"Well, I'm not doing any good at it. All I ever wanted was to be in the army. I can enlist on my own when I'm 18, but that's only a few months away. Do you think Mom and Dad would sign for me to enlist early?"

I shook my head. "Gosh, Sandy, I don't know. I guess you'll have to ask them."

Sandy did ask, and in January of 1965 he went off to boot camp. The war in Viet Nam was heating up, and Sandy had hopes of going over. He hoped he'd finish his training before the skirmishes were over. Before he left, he'd asked his girlfriend, Sharyn, to wait for him. He wanted to marry her.

I wasn't ready for that kind of seriousness, so that spring I decided to take a set of twins to the prom. I was dating Lynn, but her sister, Lee, didn't date very much. They did everything together, and so I just boldly asked them both to go with me.

I had no idea how expensive prom night would be. I bought two corsages and three dinners, but I had to buy four tickets to the prom because they only came in pairs.

190

There was an all-night movie after that, and I had to pay for three tickets to that.

At the dance, I put one girl on each arm and danced with them both at the same time. Other kids kept coming up and singing the Doublemint gum commercial: "Double your pleasure, double your fun . . . . " I told them to get lost.

By the fall after I graduated from high school, Sandy had been sent to Germany. I had missed being with him every time he was home on leave, and we just hadn't had any time together. Sandy's letters showed that the army was changing him—helping him grow up. He didn't need me to protect him anymore. But I never really got to see any of that. My best buddy was a continent and an ocean away.

Although Sandy had volunteered several times for service in Viet Nam, his orders never came. While I was in high school, I'd received my draft notice, and I was scheduled to report right around my dad's birthday, in November of 1965.

One day late in October my speech teacher, Larry Bird, went with me to a speaking engagement in San Bernardino. About 6:00 in the afternoon we pulled into Apple Valley. As we headed down our block, I noticed the driveway full of cars. I felt uneasy.

"Larry," I said slowly, "Mom's supposed to fly in from Texas tonight. It's her birthday. I hope everything's okay. Mom's had more than one near-miss, flying."

We walked into the living room, and I saw Linda and Dodie, and our pastor, Bill Hanson. Then I spotted Dad. He was sitting in a chair with his elbows resting on his knees. His face buried in his hands, he was sobbing.

"Dusty," somebody said, "something's happened to Sandy. He's dead."

191

Dead? What kind of horrible joke is that? But I knew it was true. We were waiting for further reports, but the first word was, my brother had choked to death in Germany.

"It's time to go. We have to meet Mom at the airport so no one tells her before we can," Linda said. We climbed into several cars and drove out to Los Angeles International Airport. We stood around waiting, and then we saw the plane taxi in.

"How am I ever going to tell her?" Dad asked Reverend Bill.

"Do you want me to?"

Dad shook his head. "No. I'll take care of it."

But no one had to say a word. The minute Mom got off the plane and saw us all standing there, she knew.

"Oh, my God," she cried, "not Sandy! Not Sandy! He's in Germany, not Viet Nam!" Suddenly her legs went out from under her, and Dad grabbed her. A couple of security men rushed over, and they helped us into a small private room. Mom was hysterical for nearly two hours.

In the days that followed, we learned the circumstances that surrounded Sandy's death. To celebrate the completion of some maneuvers, the guys in Sandy's barracks decided to have a bash. Sandy had never had anything stronger than beer before, but he wanted so much to belong—to fit in—that he simply went along with the crowd. In a short period of time, he drank an enormous amount of alcohol—champagne, beer, whiskey, gin, vodka, brandy—all to prove himself a man.

Sandy's cast-iron stomach was never intended to handle all that poison, and he began to vomit. One of his buddies took him to the infirmary, where the doctors checked on him several times during the night. At 2:00 in the morning he seemed to be all right, and again at 3:00 he responded to the doctor, but sometime between 3:00 and 6:00 A.M., he must have begun vomiting as he lay on his back. He choked to death.

I was angry. I was angry at the senselessness of it all. Angry that Sandy had had such a tragic early childhood that he could never overcome his feelings of inferiority. Angry that God had taken him before I had time to see my brother become a man. Angry that it was Sandy who died and not me.

And the questions. *Why? Why Sandy? Why this way? Why not me? Why had he had so much against him? Why didn't God let Sandy lead the good life and take me instead?* After awhile you quit questioning. The questions drive you nuts, so you just have to let it go.

The military funeral was held at Forest Lawn, and Sandy was buried near Debbie and Robin. I'd decided that Sandy should be buried with his favorite Civil War sword, and I took it with me to the cemetery. The color guard from Ridgewood Military Academy came, and Colonel Metcalf was there. He walked with me up to the casket. I was glad, because I didn't think I could make it on my own.

I looked at Sandy, all dressed in his military uniform. *Oh, Sandy. I'll never be able to put my arms around you again. Never shake your hand. That's all I want, right now.* I reached down to put the sword into his hand; it was stiff and cold. That's when I realized that Sandy wasn't there. All the warmth, all the fun, all the stuff that was Sandy was not there at all, and suddenly I knew with certainty: Sandy was with God.

fifteen

Three days after Sandy died, I was to report for induction in San Diego. Hoping for an extension, Dad called the draft board and told them about Sandy. Because of the Sullivan Act, I was immediately reclassified 4-A, which is sole surviving son, and I did not serve in the military.

While I was attending Victor Valley High, I didn't have a regular job. Dad's museum attracted visitors daily, and I earned money by selling hand-crafted items in the gift shop. I worked a lot with casting resin. At that time, grape clusters were very popular. I also made trivets and key chains and little apples with Mom and Dad's pictures on them.

That was all right in high school, but I needed a better job. Secretly, what I really wanted to do was act. I finally got up enough courage to talk to Dad about it.

"Dad, there's nothing around here in the way of performing arts classes. The Pasadena Playhouse offers classes, and I'd really like to try my hand at it."

"Dusty, it's a hard, hard life. You've seen what it takes to be an actor. Are you sure this is what you want?"

"I think it is. The trouble is, I haven't been able to earn much money, and I can't afford to go to Pasadena on my own. The lessons are very expensive. Would you be willing to help?"

Dad leaned back in his chair and looked at me intently. "Dusty, I'm not willing to make an investment like that unless you're absolutely sure it's what you want. We could send you on a trial basis to see how you do, but I don't want to make a long-term commitment to it unless you're sure."

The words were there, but I didn't think Dad was hot on the idea, and I never brought it up again. Not long after that, Dad heard about a tool and die company in Los Angeles that was hiring, so I went down and took a test. Apparently I scored the highest marks they had ever seen, and I was hired immediately. Dad was thrilled.

But I wasn't. I hated it. I loved to be outside, but my job was indoors, stuck in a place that was dark and dank and greasy. I enjoyed being creative, but there was nothing creative about my work. My first job was testing seams on napalm bombs destined for Viet Nam, to make sure they didn't leak.

The more I worked, the more I thought about those bombs. I remembered the terror that had shaken Debbie when we were discussing the Cuban Missile Crisis, and I just couldn't see myself contributing to that. I asked my boss for a different assignment.

To be put into another position, I had to have high security clearance, and when that came, I was put to work grinding little round rings with wings on them. My job was to grind the wings to a very sharp edge. I thought they were bearings for truck parts, until I made a discovery.

Those deadly little metal pieces were put inside land mines. When the enemy hit a trip wire, those things came out of the ground about belly level and exploded. The wings wound themselves into the person. Sick at the thought of it, I quit.

Unlike many of my contemporaries, I was no dove. Like my parents, I believed we had a responsibility to be in Viet Nam, but it seemed to us that we were going about it all wrong. So many lives were at stake, I kept wondering why we were messing around. Why didn't we just do the job or get out?

At the same time, I couldn't handle the napalm business, and making weapons that were designed to maim. I was also feeling restless. Even before Sandy died, Dad and I had begun to drift apart. Looking back, I realize now that much of what was happening was the natural process of growing up, getting ready to leave the nest. Part of it was our own private grief. But part of it was a lack of communication.

Although Dad had spent most of his life in front of audiences, entertaining thousands of people at a time, he was—and is—painfully shy. It's difficult for him to express his feelings. The grief of those years compounded that, and our communication level dropped.

"Dad's never here for me anymore, Mom," I said one day.

"Yes, he is, Dusty," she answered. "You two just need to talk to each other, that's all. Just the other day he told me that you're never here for him!"

"Can't you tell him . . . "

"Dusty, I'll tell you what I told him. I'm not going to be

the interpreter for the two of you. I won't do that. You need to talk to each other."

But it didn't work that way. I told Mom what I was thinking and feeling, and Dad told her, but we didn't tell each other. We had begun to draw conclusions by what we saw and what we thought we heard, instead of talking to each other. I respected him, and he respected me, but it seemed like we were always standing on the outside of the window, looking in.

When I quit working for the tool and die maker, Dad was furious. He never said so, but it seemed to me he was thinking I'd blown my opportunity for a decent future. I'd have done anything to avoid disappointing him, but he was deeply disappointed in me anyway. I couldn't stand that.

Figuring it would blow over if I laid low for awhile, I headed for Ohio to visit friends. Once there, I decided to stay. Only recently did the irony hit me. When he was 18, Dad set out for California from Ohio; I was 19, and doing the same thing in reverse!

In Ohio I went to work for a construction company. We were building homes and factories from the ground up. I learned to run a back hoe, a front-end loader, a skip loader, and a grader. I used a chain saw to clear woods, and I pulled stumps. I laid blocks, framed houses, set shingles, hung drywall, and installed plumbing.

While I was learning the construction business, I met the prettiest little blonde girl, who turned out to be my boss's daughter. Linda was barely 5'2", and I was stretching 6'4". My friend Terry White knew her, and he told me she was going to be in the senior class play at the high school.

I asked him if she had a steady boyfriend, and he said no.

"Are you sure?"

"I'm sure. She's not going with anyone."

"Do you think she'd go out with me?"

So the fool went and asked her, but not before he spread it all over the school. Naturally she said no because I didn't have the guts to ask her myself.

The opening night of the play I sent her two dozen red roses with a note:

> Linda,
>
> I'm sorry Terry and I embarrassed you. If you ever need a tag-along for a date, I'd be glad to go.
>
> Dusty Rogers

The next thing I knew, she was coming down the hall toward me. She walked up to me, and I leaned down as she stood on her tiptoes and kissed me on the cheek.

"Thank you for the roses!"

I stumbled all over myself, apologizing again, and suddenly a fellow came up and started telling Linda off for two-timing him! He told her he wouldn't take her to the cast party—so I went instead.

That was in April, and in August I called my folks to tell them Linda and I wanted to get married in November.

"Oh, Dusty," Dad groaned. "Why an Ohio girl? Why not a California girl?" It was my first hint that he really wanted me to be closer, that he missed me.

Why Linda? She was tiny, but she could certainly hold her own. Outgoing and articulate, she seemed sure of herself. Although she was only 18, she was solid and down-to-earth. She wasn't the least bit impressed with my family name, and she loved me for myself. Though we couldn't have been more opposite in temperament and personality, I loved her. Still do.

A few days after my call Mom and Dad sent a letter

giving us their blessing. Finally the day arrived. Our wedding was the event of the season in our little Ohio town, and the local newspapers made so much of it that the wire services picked it up. The papers made the most of the fact that Dad and Mom were the King of the Cowboys and the Queen of the West, and the headlines read, "Local Girl Marries Royalty!" Linda and I have a scrapbook filled with clippings from all over the country.

We had a huge church wedding, and Mom and Dad flew back with Dodie for the ceremony. Linda's father had grown up among the Amish, so it was quite a scene. There was the Roy Rogers and Dale Evans clan, and Linda's mom's family, and her dad's family all decked out in their finest black. Newspaper photographers had a heyday with that, and when the photos appeared in the papers, the captions read, "Old Meets New."

Because of the publicity, we received cards and letters and gifts from all over the country. Some of them arrived addressed simply, "Mr. and Mrs. Roy Rogers, Jr., Middlefield, Ohio." Because people loved Mom and Dad so much, they wanted to remember us as well. Linda and I were touched by that, and by the people who came. Dad's high school teacher drove all the way from southern Ohio, and other friends came from as far away as California.

Those early years of our marriage were tough. Mom and Dad let me make my own way, as they had with my sisters. Although I knew they would help if I asked, I never did. We lived in a little mobile home that froze our bones in winter and boiled our blood in summer, and when Linda became pregnant, I swept floors at a local supermarket at night in exchange for baby food.

We stayed in Ohio for 10 years, and our daughters, Kelly and Shawna, were born there. I worked in the construction business, and on the side I made personal

Our wedding day, November 18, 1967.

My family today. (Clockwise from top left) Linda,
Shawna, Dustin, Kelly and me.

appearances and sang. For awhile I had my own television show, and I was also a radio disc jockey.

Finally, after a particularly hard winter, I told Linda my blood would never thicken enough for me to enjoy the Ohio winters. I wanted to go back to California, so we packed our bags and moved back to Apple Valley. I went right to work as a construction supervisor.

Our son, Dustin, was born while I earned my contractor's license and started building custom homes. I built Mom and Dad a new place, and I'm very proud of it. Off and on I did some singing, and in 1982 I formed my own Country-Western band, the High Riders.

In the meantime, Dodie had grown up and was married, and Mom and Dad were alone. I'd never tried to bridge the chasm between Dad and me. It took another tragedy to make me do anything about it.

The morning of October 8, we received the news that Linda's brother, Ron, had been killed in an automobile accident. As I watched her struggle with her grief, I realized how much of it was tied to "what might have been."

"If only I'd told him I loved him more often," Linda lamented. "Now it's too late."

Linda's despair plunged her deeper and deeper into depression. I knew exactly how she felt and what her thoughts were, because I'd felt the same about Sandy and Debbie and Robin. It was as though we'd been robbed of the opportunity to express our love as fully as we really wanted to.

I tried to be sensitive to Linda, but as the days wore on, it finally reached the point that I knew a tougher stand was necessary, or we'd lose her, too.

"Linda, we need you here, now, in the present. You have a family to consider. I loved Ron, too, but he's gone, and there's nothing we can do to change that. Ron would not appreciate you sitting around here and making life miserable for everyone else. This has to stop."

She looked up at me and burst into tears. We sat and cried together for about an hour, and during the next weeks, Linda gradually began to emerge from her grief. But the more I thought about it, the more it hit home that my dad was approaching his seventies. We might not have all that much time together.

One day I climbed into my truck and drove over to the house.

"Hi, Dusty!" Dad called.

"Hi, Dad. What are you doing?"

"Just heading out to buy some trees."

"Care for some company?"

"Sure. Come along." We made small talk for awhile, and then he looked at me kind of sideways and said, "You got something on your mind, son?"

I nodded. "I'm scared, Dad."

He looked at me, concerned. "Scared? What's eating at you, Dusty?"

"You know, Dad, we've been father and son for over 30 years, and you've been a great dad. But we've never really been buddies, and that's bothered me."

That set him back a bit. He stared at me for a few moments, and then he said, "It *has* been a long time since we really talked."

"A long time? Dad, we've *never* talked. I'm afraid. It really frightens me that one day I'll wake up and you'll be gone, and we'll never have had the chance to really know each other. You know, I never told Ron how much I loved and appreciated him. I don't want that day to come for you and me."

Dad was quiet for a few seconds. "Dusty, that bothers me, too." He pulled the truck over to the side of the road, and we got out and walked through the field.

"Dad, I've always been afraid of disappointing you. I *hated* thinking I'd disappoint you. But when something bothers you, you never say anything. I just don't know where I stand!"

"Well, you know son, that's just how I was raised. I just keep it inside."

"I do, too. But that's no way to be. If you don't tell me, how can I know if what I do is acceptable?"

He looked at me a minute. "You know when you were building the house and you said you'd come over and take that sign down?"

I nodded.

"Well, you never did. I had to tear it down myself."

For Dad to share something that would seem insignificant to most people was like a gift to me, and for the next hour, we told each other our pet peeves and what we like and what we don't.

Finally, I knew we had aired our feelings—not just our disappointments, but positive feelings, too. I looked at Dad. He stood there, shyly.

"I love you, Dad," I said.

"I love you, Son," he whispered. We wrapped our arms around each other, then turned and strolled back to the truck.

From that day on, we have never let a day pass without an embrace, without saying, "I love you." That conversation made all the difference in the world to us. It solidified in us the reality that fame and fortune mean nothing if we are impoverished in our relationships with those who mean the most to us.

Not long after that discussion, I had the opportunity to do something I'd been wanting to do for a long time. The High Riders and I were asked to do a concert at the Holi-

204

day Inn over in Victorville. In our show we sing a lot of Country-Western songs, I do a monologue, and we finish up with a "Pioneer Medley," singing some of the songs that Dad and the Sons of the Pioneers made famous.

On the radio one day, I heard a song about John Wayne. *How sad,* I thought, *to write a song for somebody after he's gone and can't appreciate it. Why can't Dad have a song of his own, right now?* I tried, but I couldn't seem to make it work, so I went to Larry Carney, who is my bass player.

"I've got some of the words, Larry," I explained, "but I need a better hook. Dad's a living legend. People love him, and they know his trademarks. Let's write a song that focuses on his horse and his hat and so on, but doesn't mention his name."

Larry worked on it, and it sounded great to me. For a week before the concert, I was all nerves, but I told Mom I wanted Dad to be there. The night of the performance 400 people came, and I couldn't bring myself to talk to my parents. I saw them in the audience, and when we finished the Pioneer Medley, I stepped up to the microphone.

"Ladies and gentlemen," I said, "I have a song I'd like to share with you. It's never been sung in public before, and I'd like to dedicate it to my dad."

The song talks about the kind and gentle living legend that has touched our lives for more than 40 years:

> And I know forever,
> In many hearts he'll reign
> As the King of the Cowboys,
> There is honor to his name.

I've never had a tougher time singing. Every time I looked at Dad, he was teary, and when I finished, the entire audience was on its feet. The applause was like thunder.

"Dad, this is for you. They really love you," I said. "I really love you, too."

Finally he stood up. The applause went on for a full five minutes. I watched him as he nodded shyly at the people who were celebrating him, and inside, I celebrated, too. Yes, the odds had been against us all, but God had overcome the odds. It was one of the best nights of my life.

CHRISTIAN HERALD ASSOCIATION AND ITS MINISTRIES

CHRISTIAN HERALD ASSOCIATION, founded in 1878, publishes The Christian Herald Magazine, one of the leading interdenominational religious monthlies in America. Through its wide circulation, it brings inspiring articles and the latest news of religious developments to many families. From the magazine's pages came the initiative for CHRISTIAN HERALD CHILDREN and THE BOWERY MISSION, two individually supported not-for-profit corporations.

CHRISTIAN HERALD CHILDREN, established in 1894, is the name for a unique and dynamic ministry to disadvantaged children, offering hope and opportunities which would not otherwise be available for reasons of poverty and neglect. The goal is to develop each child's potential and to demonstrate Christian compassion and understanding to children in need.

Mont Lawn is a permanent camp located in Bushkill, Pennsylvania. It is the focal point of a ministry which provides a healthful "vacation with a purpose" to children who without it would be confined to the streets of the city. Up to 1000 children between the age of 7 and 11 come to Mont Lawn each year.

Christian Herald Children maintains year-round contact with children by means of a *City Youth Ministry.* Central to its philosophy is the belief that only through sustained relationships and demonstrated concern can individual lives be truly enriched. Special emphasis is on individual guidance, spiritual and family counseling and tutoring. This follow-up ministry to inner-city children culminates for many in financial assistance toward higher education and career counseling.

THE BOWERY MISSION, located at 227 Bowery, New York City, has since 1879 been reaching out to the lost men on the Bowery, offering them what could be their last chance to rebuild their lives. Every man is fed, clothed and ministered to. Countless numbers have entered the 90-day residential rehabilitation program at the Bowery Mission. A concentrated ministry of counseling, medical care, nutrition therapy, Bible study and Gospel services awakens a man to spiritual renewal within himself.

These ministries are supported solely by the voluntary contributions of individuals and by legacies and bequests. Contributions are tax deductible. Checks should be made out either to CHRISTIAN HERALD CHILDREN or to THE BOWERY MISSION.

Administrative Office: 40 Overlook Drive, Chappaqua, New York 10514
Telephone: (914) 769-9000